Object Success

Object Success

A Manager's Guide to Object Orientation, its Impact on the Corporation, and its Use for Reengineering the Software Process

Bertrand Meyer

ISE Inc.
Santa Barbara, California

Prentice Hall

London   New York   Toronto   Sydney   Tokyo   Singapore
Madrid   Mexico City   Munich

First published 1995 by
Prentice Hall International (UK) Ltd
Campus 400, Maylands Avenue
Hemel Hempstead
Hertfordshire, HP2 7EZ

A division of
Simon & Schuster International Group

Printed and bound in Great Britain by T.J. Press Ltd, Padstow.

Library of Congress Cataloging-in-Publication Data

Available from the publisher

British Library Cataloguing in Publication Data

A catalogue record for this book is available from
the British Library

ISBN: 0-13-192833-3

---

2   3   4   5   99   98   97   96   95

Contents

Interactive
Software Engineering Inc.

Mr. Cuthbert D. Highbrows III
President and Chief Executive Officer
The Cresus-Midas Group International
One Cresus-Midas Crescent
Boston, MA 01431

April 15, 1995

Dear Cuth:

Please find enclosed the report on "Objects for Business" that you commissioned from our company. As you will see, I have retitled it *Object Success* to emphasize how a Fortune 500 corporation such as CMGI can profit from object technology to re-engineer its business process. It relies on two decades of experience in developing object-oriented tools, libraries and applications, teaching the method in both industrial and academic environments, and providing management and technical consulting to many O-O projects around the world.

You may recall that during our first conversation on this subject last summer you asked: "What's all this object stuff about?". I replied, perhaps a bit brashly: "It is not about objects; it is about abstraction". You remarked that with the possible exception of TV preachers you hadn't heard of anyone ever getting rich by selling abstractions, and you challenged me to produce a report that would enable any high- or middle-manager at Cresus-Midas to relate to object technology in terms of his or her career. You also encouraged me to respect no sacred cow; "debunk" is one of the words I remember.

Well, here it is. Because "objects" are a technical topic I have included just enough technical material to enable a serious discussion, but most of the text is about economic and managerial issues. Please distribute this as widely as you wish to your management.

By separate mail I am sending you the invoice for this work, according to our contract. By the way — I hate to bother you with this, but could you check that we get paid diligently this time? We have not yet been reimbursed for our expenses in connection with the previous report, and the purchasing department is all on voice mail and does not return our calls. Thanks for devoting your attention to this matter.

I hope this report will enable Cresus-Midas to gain from object technology the competitive edge that it amply deserves. Preparing this report has been a greatly rewarding experience; I especially enjoyed all the interaction with you and your superb staff. You sure know how to surround yourself with the best people in the business.

I hope there will be further opportunities to collaborate. Please do not hesitate to contact me should you wish to expand this work or simply to discuss it.

Yours sincerely,

Bertrand Meyer

Object-Oriented Excellence

270 Storke Road Suite 6 Goleta CA 93117 USA— Telephone 805.685.1006 — Fax 805.685.6869

1

Object frenzy

The February 7, 1994, issue of *ComputerWorld* — the weekly hope of data processing executives who try to figure out where their industry may be going — is a typical one in all respects. It has the usual mix of announcements and counter-announcements: Apple *plans* to emulate Windows on its *planned* new machines; IBM plans to introduce a symmetrical multiprocessing workstation; Digital plans to introduce a four-processor superserver and, in a separate story, plans to add clustering software; Novell plans to release a foundation application development environment.

And "objects" are on almost every page.

One company has "an object-oriented framework that monitors Unix systems". Another is planning a "hybrid object/relational database". Some developers are said to voice concerns about Microsoft's "Object Linking and Embedding", for which they must develop "little chunks of code, in the form of objects, that allow developers to, for example, insert a spreadsheet into an application". Competing "object frameworks" from Hewlett-Packard and SunSoft will not be able to interoperate until an outfit that calls itself the "Object Management Group" releases its planned 2.0 document. Computer Associates International's planned "CA-Visual Objects for Windows" recently entered beta testing. SunSoft plans to add "object class libraries" from Next Step to its "Distributed Objects Everywhere" project.

What is the typical MIS executive to do under such a deluge? How does one distinguish the product from the plan, the serious from the fanciful, the concept from the buzzword, the ware from the vapor?

Not easy. But if ObjectSpeak confuses you, do not despair: you are not alone. People who have been practicing object technology for years feel just as dizzy, and in fact some of those who *invented* the concepts do not necessarily fare much better. Objects may be Distributed Everywhere, in the press at least, but it is not always clear what all this means for the software manager who has deadlines to meet and customers to please.

This book is intended for such people. It explains in simple terms what object technology is about and, just as importantly, what it is not about. It presents the technology (mostly in chapter 2 and the Appendix) but talks more about what it means for corporations in terms of profits, costs, workflow, team organization, long-term plans and short-term effects. It shows the promises of object technology but also explores the areas of risk. In short, it is a pragmatic, down-to-earth presentation what the technology means from an enterprise perspective; it discards object frenzy and discusses the business of objects.

WHAT IS IT REALLY ABOUT?

The first step to find out when assessing a new device or a new technology is what it is trying to solve. An Espresso machine is not for hashing potatoes.

For object technology it is particularly important to define precisely what we are looking for. Over the years successive waves of newcomers have been sold on the merits of object orientation in widely different ways, each of which was dominant for two or three years. Here is a partial list with approximate dates:

- As an Artificial Intelligence technique (1980-82).

- As an environment for developing fancy user interfaces (1983-86).

- As a prototyping mechanism (1987-88).

- As a way to modernize the C programming language (1989-90).

- As a tool for analysis and design (1991-92).

- As a mechanism for exchanging some data over a computer network (the latest craze, well reflected in the above *ComputerWorld* extracts: 1993-?).

Seeing this, a casual observer might be tempted to ask "Sure, and does it make coffee too?" This would in fact be unfair since object technology, remarkably, *is* in fact applicable in all the ways mentioned. But none of them captures the essence of the technology; instead they all are *consequences* of its main properties.

What the object-oriented method really addresses is at the same time more mundane and more far-reaching than any of the above: object orientation is a **software engineering** technique.

Software engineering here is simply defined as the study of methods and tools that can be used to produce quality practical software. (The term, although perhaps imperfect, is the accepted one. We will have the opportunity to discuss how much the "engineering" part of it is appropriate; for the moment please accept the name as a shorthand for the definition just given.) Two key aspects of this definition are the role of *quality* and the emphasis on *practical* software — software that is meant for operational use and is developed under the usual economic and organizational constraints of industrial environments.

Object orientation provides a set of powerful concepts to address some of the most pressing problems of software quality. Its most exciting contribution affects in particular the following aspects of quality:

- **Reliability** — the ability to produce bug-free systems (and systems that work *the first time around*).

- **Extendibility** — the ability to produce software that can be adapted at reasonable effort when external requirements or technical constraints change.

- **Reusability** — the ability to build a system from pre-existing parts, and to make sure that *its* own parts can serve again for future developments.

- **Portability** — the ability to produce software that can be moved to various hardware-software platforms at no undue cost.

- **Efficiency** — the ability to produce high-performance software.

As anyone with experience in the software industry knows, these are among the most pressing needs that the field currently faces, and it is exciting to know that one specific approach to software construction has so much to offer to approach them.

QUALITY VERSUS PRODUCTIVITY?

In the past thirty years, before object technology captured the attention of the software industry, many ideas had been introduced to improve the state of software, from general concepts (starting with structured programming as early as 1968) to specific methods, languages and tools. In most cases the arguments for these approaches emphasized *productivity*. The goals listed above for object technology, and for software engineering in general, emphasize *quality*. Does this mean that we must forsake the idea of improving software productivity through object-oriented techniques?

No. Typical productivity is unsatisfactory in today's software development — software just costs more to develop and maintain than it should — and object technology can help improve it considerably. The question, however, is to set the right priority.

Many tools are available that make it possible to produce software faster. But that is not the major problem facing the software industry; a more important matter is what happens after a first version has been produced. As discussed more extensively in the following chapters, this is where most of the software efforts and costs go. So the concern for quality is not exclusive of the concern for productivity: the best way to decrease software costs is to ensure that products are of good quality in the first place. In the words of K. Fujino, a Vice President of NEC Corporation of Japan, *"when quality is pursued, productivity will follow"* (quoted in the book by Ghezzi et al., see the bibliography at the end of this chapter).

Such productivity benefits are not immediate. What about the short term? Our experience at ISE and that of our customers indicates that a group that masters object technology has a considerable edge — when it comes to putting out a product to market quickly and effectively— over one using traditional approaches. The effects on productivity are almost as impressive as those on quality.

But the qualification given is essential: the team must *master object technology*. This normally will not apply to the first project undertaken by a team; as with any new approach, some productivity will be lost because of the need to come to terms with an unfamiliar approach, a new language, new tools; inevitably, some mistakes will be made and some time will be lost, negating some of the advantages of the approach.

Whether the positive contributions will yield an immediate productivity improvement anyway, or whether the initial difficulties will supersede them for the first project — that is impossible to say in the general case. Soon after, the productivity advantages of object technology should become obvious anyway. But for anyone in charge of introducing the approach into a company these observations suggest a key rule (which will also influence the proper handling of pilot projects, studied in chapter 5): be sure to advertize object technology for its true contributions.

Promoting the approach for its quality benefits may make the initial sell a bit tougher, because productivity is what most corporate executives — tired of the costs and delays that software typically evokes for them — will want to hear about. But it avoids the risk of a backlash if the first project does not immediately show a tenfold increase in productivity. It defines the right mindset for *object success* within the corporation: focusing on producing software that is of much higher quality than before. And it can only yield pleasant surprises when the productivity benefits do become visible.

EXPECTATIONS AND REALITY

The claims routinely made on behalf of object technology suggest two caveats and a counter-caveat.

Caveat 1: the quality factors listed above are not all that matters for software engineering, and indeed object orientation leaves some aspects untouched — neither better nor worse than what they were before.

Caveat 2: for those issues that the technology does address, it does not *solve* them; it simply helps progress towards a solution. Software construction is a tough problem, and one should not expect miracles.

But if overselling object orientation is absurd it would be equally wrong to use this observation as a reason to dismiss the technology. Perhaps the most damaging contribution here is an often quoted article by Fred Brooks (see the reference at the end of this chapter) which completely missed the originality of object technology, treating it as just another potentially interesting idea. The article's title, *No Silver Bullet*, was immediately seized by anyone who had a vested interest in maintaining the software status quo, and whenever a company or university starts considering object-oriented methods you can expect some well-meaning soul to circulate photocopies of that article.

This leads us to the *counter-caveat*: do not hype the technology, but do no underestimate its potential. If practiced seriously and competently, it can yield tremendous improvements in the software process and the resulting products. When we come to studying experiences from actual object-oriented projects, we will encounter, in chapter 5, a quote from the manager of a large, commercially successful object-oriented project: "OOP holds *more* promise than the current hype would have us believe" (see page 87).

Most managers know the risk of embracing new ideas too soon; good managers also know the risk of embracing them too late.

BIBLIOGRAPHY

Fred P. Brooks: *No Silver Bullet: Essence and Accidents of Software Engineering*, in *Computer* (IEEE), 20, 4, April 1987, pp. 10-20

> A general discussion of the difficulty of software development, with a cursory review (a few paragraphs each) of various techniques for approaching the problem, such as time-sharing (hardly a breakthrough in 1987), expert systems, automatic programming, unified programming environments, Ada and object-oriented programming, leading to the breathtaking conclusion that there is no instant solution and that what we need most is bright designers.

Carlo Ghezzi, Mehdi Jazayeri, Dino Mandrioli: *Fundamentals of Software Engineering*, Prentice Hall, 1991.

> A comprehensive introduction to modern concepts of software engineering

2

The ten key O-O concepts

To introduce object technology successfully into an organization, you must, even if you are a manager rather than a software professional, have a basic understanding of what the method is about: what aspects of software construction it affects, and what aspects it leaves unchanged.

Because you are probably eager to get to the managerial aspects analyzed in the following chapters, the more technical part of the discussion has been kept for the end of this book — the Appendix, starting on page 155. The present chapter focuses on ten ideas that stand at the center of object technology. It also touches on a few complementary points such as the role of O-O languages, O-O databases and O-O analysis. Except for a couple of extracts illustrating the look-and-feel of major O-O languages, this chapter shows no actual software texts; but it will equip you with enough technical background to follow the non-technical discussions of subsequent chapters. I do hope that it will pique your interest, leading you to read the Appendix (which contains a few actual software examples) and perhaps, later on, some of the more in-depth books cited in the bibliography.

As everything else in this book, the discussion will study the ideas as seen through a manager's eyes. One of the most remarkable properties of the method is indeed how close some of its principal metaphors — client, supplier, contract, dependency, decentralization, information hiding... — are to the concepts of business life. These analogies are particularly important to managers, and the discussion will emphasize them throughout.

THE GOALS

Before exploring our Ten Key Concepts let us take a closer look at the goals of the technology introduced in the previous chapter. We saw the major quality factors that the method is meant to improve: reusability, extendibility, reliability, portability and efficiency. For the first four, where the method's contribution is the most significant, the ultimate incentive is really the same, summarized by a general observation:

> ### THE BASIC ISSUE OF SOFTWARE CONSTRUCTION
>
> If you think writing software is difficult, try *re*writing software.

The largest part of the software industry's efforts — 60% to 80% according to various studies — is devoted not to producing software systems but to modifying them after they have already been put together. Developers have a cynical saying — "there is never time to do it right, but there is always time to do it over" — to describe this situation. The preceding statement of the Basic Issue is more constructive, and points to the basic problem: modifying or correcting existing software is much more costly than getting it right in the first place. To solve this issue we need coordinated progress on all the cited quality fronts:

- Making software more reliable means decreasing later efforts at rewriting it to correct errors. Object technology will help through techniques such as static typing, Design by Contract, assertions, exception handling and garbage collection.

- Making software more extendible means decreasing later efforts at rewriting it to accommodate changes in requirements, design decisions or implementation techniques. This is perhaps the area where the contribution of object technology is the most stunning. Extendibility is a sore point of traditional methods; they tend to produce intricate software structures, where modules are so interdependent that a modification anywhere may trigger a chain reaction of changes throughout the system. In contrast, the decentralized architecture of object-oriented systems allows you to change your mind without being punished too hard for your hesitations.

- Making software more reusable means that you can avoid rewriting variants of software elements that you or others have written before. Some cases are trivial: any method will let you reuse a software element to solve a problem identical to what the element originally addressed. The significant issues of reusability arise when you try to reuse an element to cover a similar but slightly different need. This is where object technology will make a difference, by allowing you to combine reuse with adaptation.

- Making software more portable means decreasing the effort needed to adapt it to a new operating system or to a new hardware architecture.

All this also illustrates the positive effect of quality on productivity, discussed at the end of the preceding chapter: fewer errors, easier changes, more reuse and more portable systems will all help decrease software development costs.

The techniques sketched in the rest of this chapter and the Appendix help reach these goals. Some of them may look surprising at first, especially since it is not the role of this book to go into detailed technical justifications (which may, however, be found in some of the books quoted in the bibliography). These techniques, as well as many of the concepts discussed in later chapters, all address the Basic Issue of software construction.

> Among the goals listed, one deserves repeated emphasis: reliability. One of the most traumatic aspects of developing software and (particularly) managing its development, is the problem of errors. Software engineering textbooks do not talk much about this aspect; yet errors, or bugs as they are more commonly called, plague the whole process. Particularly vexing is the ever-present possibility that an unexpected bug will suddenly come up and cause days or weeks of aggravation. In my experience with the version of object technology that we use, progress on that front has been one of the most rewarding confirmations of the validity of the approach. Bugs remain, but they tend to be *design* bugs: forgotten cases, results of incorrect reasoning, wrong assumptions about the environment. The low-level bugs, which can at times make traditional programming nightmarish, all but disappear — with one exception: the small and decreasing part of our software that we must keep written in C as an interface to other tools, accounting for a disproportionate share of the development problems. In the part that is truly object-oriented, the reliability benefits, and the way they affect the software process, would by themselves provide enough justification for using this technology.

CONCEPT ONE: ARCHITECTURE

> ## ARCHITECTURE PRINCIPLE
>
> Object technology primarily affects the architecture of software systems.

Everything other than architecture — fancy development environments, networking, analysis, databases — is either supporting technology or a consequence.

The architecture of a software system is defined here as its organization into coherent pieces, or **modules,** and the description of how these modules interact with each other. A useful software engineering concept is the distinction between *programming-in-the-small,* covering the atomic constituents of programs, such as instructions, expressions and the like, and *programming-in-the-large,* covering the high-level groupings of these elements. The architecture of a system comprises its in-the-large properties.

Why the focus on architecture? The reason may be found in the goals that have been defined for object technology. To make software extendible and reusable what will count most is the flexibility of its structure and the autonomy of its modules. To make it reliable, you will also need to ensure that the architecture is as simple as possible. Complexity is the fiercest enemy of reliability.

CONCEPT TWO: CLASSES

> ## CLASS PRINCIPLE
>
> Each basic unit of an object-oriented software system, called a class, is deduced from one of the types of data relevant to the application.

For a long time, people who build software were told to decompose their systems according to the division into operations, often known as the systems' **functions.** For example an MIS (Management Information Systems) application would be decomposed into parts corresponding to such functions as

Print invoice for international customer

The object-oriented approach reverses this perspective. Instead of functions the method focuses on data abstractions, also called classes. A class describes a type of data, specified abstractly through its external properties. For example:

• An MIS system may have a class *CUSTOMER* describing the abstract notion of customer, known through its abstract properties.

• A computer-aided design (CAD) system may have a class *ENGINE,* covering the notion of car engine described through whatever properties are meaningful to the CAD system.

• An electronic funds transfer (EFT) system may have a class *TRANSACTION* covering the notion of EFT transaction known through its abstract properties — amount, duration, sender, receiver, how to start it, how to find out when it is terminated.

• Or, to use an example where the target domain is computer-related, an operating system (OS) may have a class *DEVICE* covering the notion of device as handled by the OS.

If instead of ten concepts this chapter had to select just one, this would be it: the notion of class, with all that follows from it, defines object technology.

"But what about objects?", you may be thinking. No, you have not missed anything; the word has not yet appeared (except as part of the obligatory "object-oriented"). Objects will come soon; despite appearances they do not play a central role in the method.

CONCEPT THREE: INSTANCES

> ### INSTANCE PRINCIPLE
>
> It must be possible for a object-oriented software system, during its execution, to create an arbitrary number of data structures conforming to the description provided by a given class. Such data structures are called **instances** of the class.

A class describes a certain general category, for example the abstract notion of customer, engine, transaction, device or list. An instance of that class is a data structure representing one specific representative of that category — for example a specific customer, engine, transaction, device or list. For example an instance of class *ENGINE* is a particular engine, or more precisely its computer representation in the form of a data structure used by our CAD program at some point during one of its executions.

This is where objects fit in:

> ### DEFINITION: OBJECT
>
> An object is an instance of a class.

OBJECTS, CLASSES, AND PROPER TERMINOLOGY

Before going on to Concept Four let us take a closer look at the last few concepts. It is important to avoid two common confusions: confusion between software objects and physical objects; and confusion between objects and classes.

The first confusion is fostered by the terminology. The word "object" should not fool us: the objects we are talking about are computer data structures; they are not real-world objects. For example an instance of class *CUSTOMER* is not a customer — remember that according to the Instance Principle our software can **create** such instances, and we are not

Dr. Frankenstein! What we will create is much more boring than a real customer, but also more directly related to the purposes of software engineering: a data structure, to be stored in the memory of a computer, that describes our software's view of a certain customer.

There is an explanation, if not an excuse, for the confusion. Object technology provides a powerful modeling technique precisely because it is able to map concepts from the external system being modeled — be it the operation of a company, an industrial design process, the transfer of money over a network or the structure of a computer system — to software concepts. This mapping reduces the gap (the *impedance mismatch*, as it is called in a later chapter) between problem and solution, that is to say, between the eventual users of our software systems and their developers; this follows in particular from the presence of classes that model external concepts, such as *CUSTOMER* and the like, which are particularly precious for object-oriented analysis.

> An example at the end of this chapter — the sketch of a class describing the notion of vat in a chemical plant — will illustrate the technique (see page 25 and "OBJECT-ORIENTED ANALYSIS", page 31).

That object technology achieves such realism in modeling is one of its most attractive properties — which should not, however, lead us to confuse the model and the modeled. Following Magritte and his famous painting of a pipe, entitled *Ceci n'est pas une pipe* ("this is not a pipe"), we can look at a *CUSTOMER* object, that is to say an instance of class *CUSTOMER*, and assert:

> *Ceci n'est pas un customer.*

For the other frequent confusion — that between object and class — there is neither excuse nor acceptable explanation other than general sloppiness. A class is the software description of a general category of data structures, for example the notion of list; an object is one particular instance of that category, for example one list. This also means that they belong to entirely different universes. A class appears in the *text of the software*; an object is a computer data structure — in the end, a collection of zeros and ones — that exists at in the memory of a computer at some time during the execution of the software.

If we make the analogy with objects in the common, non-software sense of this term (remembering once again that this is only an analogy, and that software objects are something else than the tangible objects of daily life!), confusing classes with objects would mean confusing an abstract notion such as *COMPANY_EMPLOYEE* with one particular employee in your company — a specific instance of the concept, such as Jill whom you met this morning at the coffee machine.

All this seems rather obvious, but must be explained because the less careful part of the object-oriented literature unfortunately kindles the confusion. As a result one hears people asking for "reusable objects", meaning of course reusable classes; what is slated for reuse is the software, not one particular execution-time memory record. It is just as incorrect to say that modules in object-oriented development are based on objects: in a payroll system, you might have a class *EMPLOYEE*, providing the software view of the "employee" data abstraction; but few organizations would want a payroll program that has a module for Jill, one for you, and one for every other employee of the company!

This is more than being fussy. The object-oriented approach includes its share of intellectually challenging ideas; if we do not get the simple, unambiguous concepts right we are not likely to understand the advanced ones. And the confusion can be quite troublesome. When journalistic announcements mention (as they frequently do nowadays) the possibility for some software on a network to use "objects" elsewhere on the network, it is often hard to find out what people really mean: an operation on a machine executing an operation on an object (in the proper sense of the term) handled by another machine? Or the possibility to download classes (that is to say, software) from another machine?

The now established terminology for talking about the technology — *object-oriented* — does not help. In principle something like "class-based" or even "abstraction-based" would be better, but of course it would be futile by now to try to change such a widely accepted name. This book will rely on the usual terminology; for a bit of variety it will alternate between "object orientation", "the object-oriented method" and "object technology", with little semantic difference between these expressions. (Once or twice I might even let slip by such négligé phrasing as "Introducing objects into an organization".) What counts, however, is to avoid any confusion when discussing technical issues.

CONCEPT FOUR: RESTRICTED COMMUNICATION

> **OBJECT-ORIENTED COMMUNICATION PRINCIPLE**
>
> In a pure object-oriented approach, only two relations are permitted between classes: client and heir.

The conceptual integrity of a software system's structure, which largely determines its quality (remember the first principle: object technology is primarily about software architectures) critically depends on controlling the amount of communication that can occur between modules.

Restricting such communication — that is to say, the degree to which each may depend on others — will be essential for ensuring extendibility, reusability and reliability:

• For extendibility, dependencies mean that a change to a module may require changes to the modules on which it depends — then to those on which *they* depend, and so on.

• For reusability, dependencies mean that we cannot reuse a module without also having access to all the other modules on which it depends directly or indirectly.

• For reliability, dependencies mean potential inconsistencies and interface problems, a major source of hard-to-find bugs.

Traditional software construction techniques have failed to limit dependencies. The result, as already noted, is intricate architectures where a module may depend on many others, as in a castle of cards where removing any piece will cause the entire edifice to collapse. This is the primary reason for the lack of extendibility of much of today's software: changes requested by customers are much more difficult to carry out than they should be. The famous "application backlog" of the MIS industry is largely a consequence of this situation: if developers spend all their time painstakingly making changes to existing applications, they have no time for new ones.

At the programming language level, one of the worst causes of undue dependency is the *global variable* mechanism, which enables a module to declare a variable that many other modules, or even all other modules, can also access and set. This facility introduces tight coupling between modules and squelches any hope for decentralized software architectures.

In contrast, the object-oriented method, when fully applied, will bar global variables and only permit two relations: **client** and **heir**. A class is a client of another — its *supplier* — when it relies, for its own needs, on facilities made available by the supplier. A class is an heir of another — its *parent* — when it extends its facilities (the notion of inheritance is explored further in a subsequent section).

That is all there is to inter-module communication in proper object-oriented software construction. Classes are autonomous software elements; their dependencies on each other, if any, are explicit, and limited to the two kinds just described.

The choice of terms from the business world is of course not arbitrary. In the same way that a company cannot do everything by itself but must rely on a network of suppliers to satisfy its own clients, each class will concentrate on a well-defined job and go through other classes for everything else. To a business person, the notion of client-supplier relationship will immediately evoke the need for contracts and, sure enough, the construction of client-supplier systems will rely on *Design by Contract*, a concept introduced later in this chapter.

CONCEPT FIVE: ABSTRACTION

DATA ABSTRACTION PRINCIPLE

To make a class usable by other classes, the object-oriented method uses as sole description of the class the list of operations applicable to the corresponding instances.

The Data Abstraction Principle is key to ensuring extendibility, reusability and reliability. It holds that when a class of our software needs to use another as supplier it refuses to do so in terms of the supplier's internal properties; all that it permits itself to know is the operations, or **features**, that the supplier class has officially made available to its clients, and the officially advertized properties of these features.

Examples of features include, in a class *CUSTOMER*, operations that will provide the address of a customer, change that address, or record a sale made to the customer. In general, any operation that clients of a class may need to apply to instances of that class will be part of the features of the class.

What matters here is both what we exclude and what we include in a class description:

- A typical class will have many internal properties besides its official features; for example class *CUSTOMER* will need to include a description of the fields contained in every customer record. With traditional methods, client classes may rely on such details for their own needs. The result: any change in the internal properties of a class (as happens all the time in software development) can affect many other classes — a major source of instability and impediment to extendibility. By removing such low-level details of a class from the clients' view, we shield them from irrelevant supplier changes. This policy is known as **information hiding**; it directs the designer of any class to specify which of its properties will be accessible to its clients, and which ones — the **secrets** of the class — will be reserved for internal use.

• What we do include to describe a class is, rather than data descriptions, a specification of the applicable operations. A customer is an object to which operations such as change of address, recording a sale and others listed in the class are applicable. This list of operations entirely defines the class.

This technique of defining a type of objects solely by what you can do with them has deep consequences on the way you will build software in the object-oriented method. It continues the tradition of abstraction promoted by mathematics and other sciences, but goes further. It can be expressed by a concise general rule:

SELFISHNESS PRINCIPLE

Tell me not what you are; tell me what you can do for me.

Here the analogies with business life are almost too crying to warrant any further comment. A successful organization needs to take this cold, abstract view all the time when dealing with other organizations; it must concentrate on the essentials of any relationship — on what the partners can bring to its own business.

INFORMATION HIDING AND THE MANAGER

The terms "information hiding" and "secrets" can be misleading. In spite of its name, the principle of information hiding (which the Appendix explores in more detail in "INFORMATION HIDING", page 164) is not primarily about *preventing* the client authors from knowing the internal details of a supplier. The aim is to avoid *forcing* them to know these details.

In other words information hiding is not intended to restrain client authors but to help them; although of direct interest to managers, it is not a management tool but a development technique, whose primary purpose is to limit the amount of information that developers must learn about their suppliers when writing their own software. Without information hiding, using a module requires knowing many of its internal details; this is a huge obstacle to software reusability, since the work needed to reuse a library may be discouraging.

The absence of a strict information hiding policy is also one of the principal reasons why traditionally built software shows so little extendibility: if modules that use a module *A* may rely on any of its properties, then changing anything in *A* may require changing many other components of the system architecture. Information hiding, then, is not a matter of authoritarianism; it is a matter of survival for the developers of large systems — and especially for those who will maintain these systems.

The question remains of whether to permit client developers to know the secret parts of their supplier classes. Unlike information hiding, this is a management issue. It has no absolute answer. If the source form is available, you may or may not let client developers access it. This is not a momentous decision if the language environment that you use enforces information hiding in the proper sense of the term, that is to say if it lets supplier authors define what is exported and what is secret, and physically prevents client classes from using secret features.

When working in such an environment with developers who master the technology I have found that it is not particularly useful to add a strict secrecy discipline. Client authors will not, as a rule, *want* to read about secret details; that would simply mean adding to the mass of information that they must digest. But in some cases they may *need* this information. In particular there is always the possibility that the official documentation about a class has accidentally omitted some important piece of information.

These observations help understand the effect of an information hiding policy on the manager's role. The manager's major task is not to enforce information hiding on the client side; this will be ensured through technical rather than managerial means (by using the proper language and tools) and you may or may not let client authors find out about secret details. The more significant responsibilities for the manager are on the **supplier** side: making sure that any developer who writes a class that will be used by others carefully defines what is exported and what is not, and produces accurate interface documentation.

The last point is crucial. What can kill information hiding is not an occasional unwarranted client incursion into secret details; it is the inadequacy of supplier-side documentation, which would *compel* client authors to go look into secret information when they should not need to and, in most cases, do not want to. After a while the result would be — as when a society has too many absurd or unenforceable laws, bringing about a general disregard for all laws — to make developers distrust the principle of information hiding and revert to the use of global variables and other techniques that introduce intricate and sneaky dependencies between modules, defeating extendibility, reusability and reliability.

We will encounter a similar observation in the discussion of reusability, when noting that the difficult problems there are not on the side of the reusers, or *consumers*, but on the side of the authors of reusable modules, or *producers*. See "CHASING THE RIGHT HORSE", page 112.

CONCEPT SIX: DESIGN BY CONTRACT

> **CONTRACT PRINCIPLE**
>
> Whenever possible, the use of supplier features by a client class should be governed by a precise description of the mutual benefits and obligations.

To make client-supplier relations effective and to produce reliable software, we have to make sure, as in business relations, that the terms of the communication have been precisely established. To achieve this, authors of classes will try to associate with every applicable feature a **contract**: a detailed statement of what the feature offers to the clients, and what it requires from them in order to work properly.

As any contract between humans or companies, the contract of a feature will list mutual obligations and benefits. As is also usual, the obligations for one of the parties map into benefits for the other. Client obligations (supplier benefits) are conditions that the client must meet before calling the feature, to ensure proper execution of the feature; they are called **preconditions**. Client benefits (supplier obligations) are results that the feature must ensure; they are called **postconditions**.

Assume for example a system for managing the Frequent Flyer program of an airline (actual work around such a system serves as background for a later presentation; see "THE NOTION OF CLUSTER", page 51). One of the classes in the system could describe the notion of *MEMBER*, modeling the notion of program member. One of the features could be *promote_to_top_tier*, corresponding to a change of status applicable to very frequent travelers. The contract for this feature could look like the following:

promote_to_ top_tier	OBLIGATIONS	BENEFITS
Client	(*Satisfy precondition:*) Only call the feature for a member that has flown at least 80,000 kilometers in the current calendar year, and whose membership is in good standing.	(*From postcondition:*) Ensure that letter with coupon for 10,000 kilometers has been mailed to member, and that member is now set up to enjoy top tier privileges and promotions.
Supplier	(*Satisfy postcondition:*) Mail letter with coupon for 10,000 kilometers, and set up membership information to include top tier privileges and promotions.	(*From precondition:*) Simpler processing thanks to the assumption that proper conditions apply (enough kilometers flown, good standing).

Design by Contract is a powerful metaphor that runs through the object-oriented method. It makes it possible to design software systems of much higher reliability than ever before; the key is understanding that reliability problems (more commonly known as bugs) largely occur at module boundaries, and most often result from inconsistencies in both sides' expectations. Design by Contract promotes a much more systematic approach to this issue, by encouraging module designers to base communication with other modules on precisely defined statements of mutual obligations and benefits, not on vague hopes that everything will go right.

Such a view is particularly attractive to a manager. Information hiding provides the only possible means to remain in control of a large development; Design by Contract enables management to understand what each component of a development is trying to achieve without having to delve into the details of the component. As in business life, you use client-supplier relationships to get the job done, information hiding to ensure that each group concentrates on (and minds) its own business, and precisely worded contracts to avoid misunderstandings and disappointments.

Object-oriented languages should support these ideas by offering **assertions** that enable software writers to include the terms of software contracts (preconditions, postconditions, and also another construct known as the class invariant and explained in the Appendix) in the software text itself. Such assertions help write the software right in the first place; they provide a powerful mechanism for quality assurance, testing and (if errors remain) debugging; and they also serve as the basic documentation tool for object-oriented software, in particular reusable library classes.

CONCEPT SEVEN: INHERITANCE

> **INHERITANCE PRINCIPLE**
>
> Object-Oriented software construction makes it possible to organize related classes so as to take advantage of their commonalities and to keep the class structure understandable and manageable.

Building our systems out of classes describing data abstractions means that we may end up with many classes representing variants of the same basic notions. Inheritance allows us to organize them into well-structured hierarchies.

The Frequent Flyer system again provides an excellent example of why we need inheritance. The supporting software may have classes for the various kinds of "award" handled by the Frequent Flyer program. An award is an individual benefit that a program member will get from the program, by redeeming miles. It can be a free ticket or an upgrade — for the airline itself or for a partner airline; it can also come in the form of free car rentals, free hotel stays, or other benefits provided by the airline's partners.

In object-oriented software construction this notion of award will yield a class, since it is a proper data abstraction characterized by features; the features applicable to an *AWARD* object may include operations such as:

- *redeem*: an operation that enters all the information necessary to record that the award has been redeemed.

- *mileage_value*: an operation that returns the number of miles required for the award.

- *method_of_delivery*: an operation that returns information about how the award is to be made available to its recipient (pick up at a counter, normal mailing, express mail).

- *cancel*: an operation that cancels the award.

Because of the varieties of award kinds, we should probably use several classes: *AWARD* to describe the general notion, but also others such as *AIRLINE_AWARD*, *PARTNER_AWARD*, *NONFLIGHT_AWARD* and so on. Without inheritance these classes would probably have many similar or identical features; such redundancy would contradict the goal of reusability. With inheritance we can organize them in a proper structure reflecting their commonalities and differences:

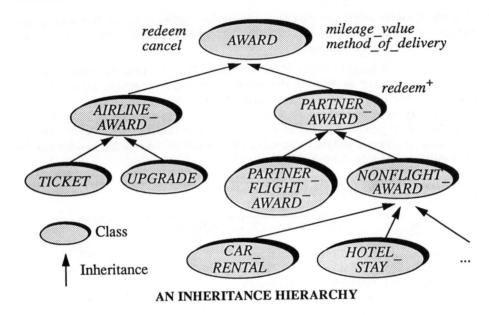

AN INHERITANCE HIERARCHY

On the figure and in the rest of the discussion, "airline award" means an award providing travel on the airline itself. Awards may also be available for travel on other airlines but they will appear under "Partner Flight Award".

Such an organization provides many advantages. It helps developers master the potential complexity of a software system, offers a sophisticated form of reusability, and opens the way to a whole new set of powerful software engineering techniques such as polymorphism and dynamic binding, reviewed next.

What is particularly interesting in the kind of reusability supported by inheritance is its flexibility. With more traditional mechanisms, such as subroutine libraries, you either reuse a component exactly as it is, or do your own development. Such inflexibility is not acceptable in software, where one frequently encounters the need to adapt to a new context. Inheritance gets us out of this **reuse or redo** dilemma. If a class inherits from one of its parents a feature whose original version is not adapted to new class's context, it can change the feature; this is called a redeclaration. For example the *redeem* operation may be different from the default mechanism for awards provided by partners; then class *PARTNER_AWARD* may redeclare feature *redeem*. This is graphically represented by the appearance of this feature with a + sign next to the class on the above figure. But the class can keep other features inherited from *AWARD* unchanged.

This ability to reconcile reusability with adaptability is one of the distinctive properties of the object-oriented method.

Also notable is the **openness** of the mechanism. Nowhere will the description of a class such as *AWARD* indicate what variants are available for the corresponding notion. The text of a class lists its parents (the classes from which it inherits); it never lists its heirs (those which inherit from it directly or indirectly). As a result, the architecture is open: it is always possible to add a new descendant to a class without affecting existing clients. This fundamental property is suggested on the preceding figure by the extra arrow and three dots below *NONFLIGHT_AWARD*, standing for all the new kinds of non-flight partner award that might later be added as the airline markets its lucrative Frequent Flyer program to new partners in various industries.

CONCEPT EIGHT: POLYMORPHISM AND DYNAMIC BINDING

> ## POLYMORPHISM AND DYNAMIC BINDING PRINCIPLE
>
> Object-oriented software construction makes it possible to build structures made of objects of different although related types, and to ensure that every operation will automatically adapt to the type of its target object.

Polymorphism is the ability to combine objects of different types into the same structure (a more precise definition appears in the Appendix). For example we may have a list of awards to be handled during a certain day; the objects of that list may be instances of different although related classes, such as *TICKET, UPGRADE, CAR_RENTAL* etc. Such a list is said to be polymorphic, that is to say many-shaped:

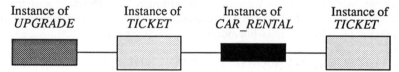

| Instance of | Instance of | Instance of | Instance of |
| *UPGRADE* | *TICKET* | *CAR_RENTAL* | *TICKET* |

A POLYMORPHIC LIST OF "AWARD" OBJECTS

Dynamic binding governs the processing of polymorphic structures. Assume that (as will probably be the case) various descendants of *AWARD* redeclare feature *redeem* in different ways, even though the figure on the preceding page only shows one such redeclaration, in class *PARTNER_AWARD*. The software may include instructions that apply this operation to every element of the list, using the general scheme

[O-O SCHEME]

> *for_every_element a apply redeem to a*

Dynamic binding here means that if the list traversal encounters objects *a* of various types, which will indeed be the case for the polymorphic list pictured above, it will automatically apply the appropriate version of *redeem* in each case: for an instance of class *TICKET*, the version of *redeem* redeclared for that class; for an instance of *UPGRADE*, the version redeclared in class *UPGRADE*; and so on. What is great about this scheme is that dynamic binding is entirely automatic: the software developers do not need to worry about adapting every feature application to the exact type of the target object; the object-oriented implementation mechanisms take care of everything.

To understand the power of this technique it suffices to think of how one would try to obtain an equivalent result in a non-object-oriented approach. The software would have to be peppered with decision structures of the form

[NON-O-O SCHEME]

*if my object represents a ticket award **then** apply the ticket version of the feature*
***else if** it is an upgrade object **then** apply the upgrade version*
***else** ...* Many more cases ...

In the text of non-object-oriented systems you will encounter this kind of construction at every street corner. It is a software engineering disaster. Not only is it heavy and tedious to write; even more importantly, it is the same for all operations that manipulate a certain polymorphic structure, meaning that if you add just one variant to the existing classes — a new kind of frequent flyer award, for example, hardly an unlikely event in the history of the software! — you will have to update **all** the elements of client software that manipulated award objects. No wonder traditional software systems are so hard to extend and maintenance accounts for such a high share of software costs.

In contrast, using the "O-O SCHEME" based on dynamic binding, you add a new class to the inheritance structure, possibly with its specific version of *redeem*, and that is all. Dynamic binding will take care of automatically applying the new mechanism to the relevant objects.

Dynamic binding may be viewed as the ultimate in abstraction and information hiding. It means that you can ignore some details not just until later stages of software construction but until the last possible moment — *execution time*.

POLYMORPHISM, DYNAMIC BINDING AND YOU

The ideas just studied are particularly relevant to the way managers see and do their job. It is often necessary for a high-level manager to give directives of the form

   "Review the security procedures for every plant"
or
   "Determine the annual bonus for every employee"
or
   "Start shareholder, analyst and press actions for the new product announcement" .

In all such cases, the directives, to be effective, must rely on the understanding that many of the requested actions have a number of possible variants, and that each affected unit will select the variant applicable to it. Each type of plant will have different security measures; each type of employee will have different bonus formula; and the public relations actions will be different for a shareholder, a Wall Street analyst and a journalist.

With old-style management, Headquarters kept a set of detailed instructions for every possible case in every possible branch of the company, similar to the complex *if... then... else if... else if...* sets of directives of old-style software architectures as illustrated in the preceding "NON-O-O SCHEME". Modern management gives more autonomy to individual units, making them responsible for implementing their specific variants of individual directives as long as they fit in the general plan defined by the corporation.

This is exactly what we obtain with redefinition, polymorphism and dynamic binding. One way to define the general plan is through assertions, which define the common framework within which each unit is free to define the variations that work best for its own context. Design by Contract is once again the guiding principle: as long as the terms of the contract are defined and accepted, it does not matter what technique each party uses to meet these terms.

The effect of object technology on the architecture of software systems is a delocalization of intelligence: instead of a central, all-encompassing center that decides everything for everyone, we try, in the interest of extendibility and reusability, to empower each module with enough information and processing power to deal with the requests addressed specifically to it. This evolution mirrors the evolution of the many excellence-seeking companies that aim for collective success by making each unit responsible for achieving its specific goals within a common general framework

The combination of client-supplier relations, polymorphism, Design by Contract and dynamic binding also evokes the normal business procedure of farming out some operations to contractors: you rely on some other company to do some work for you (client-supplier relation); for safety and flexibility, you give yourself the possibility of going to any one of several such contractors (polymorphism); you let each contractor do the job according to its own procedures and mode of operation (dynamic binding) as long as it meets the contractually specified obligations (Design by Contract). Note the importance of the last point: without specifications that guarantee consistency of the results from various suppliers, it would be very difficult to benefit from the flexibility afforded by the choice of supplier.

CONCEPT NINE: STATIC TYPING

STATIC TYPING PRINCIPLE

Object-oriented software construction should make it possible to associate a type with every entity of the software text, so as to enable compilers or other tools to check, before execution, that objects will always be able to execute the operations applied to them during execution.

The concern here is reliability. With the power of polymorphism and dynamic binding, a potential risks exists of execution-time disasters. What if the execution tries to apply a feature such as *redeem* to an object that has no such feature, for example an instance of class *MEMBER* (you cannot redeem a member of the Frequent Flyer program!) or *CITY*?

The solution is, in its basic form, straightforward. For any entity of the software text that represents execution-time objects, you must include a **declaration** that specifies the possible types (classes) for the associated objects. For example you may declare a certain entity as being of type *AWARD*. Then a feature application on the entity is valid only if it uses a feature of that class. If not, the tools of the environment, for example the compiler, will produce an error message, forcing the developers to correct the inconsistency.

Without polymorphism and dynamic binding, the static typing policy might be too constraining. But the combination of these mechanisms yields the right mix of flexibility and safety. By declaring an entity as being of type *AWARD*, you restrain its possible execution-time values, excluding for example objects of type *MEMBER* or *CITY*, but thanks to polymorphism you still leave a lot of manoeuvering room: the attached objects may be of any type that is a descendant of *AWARD*, for example *TICKET, CAR_RENTAL* or any new variant that may be added tomorrow or ten years from now.

The combination of static typing and dynamic binding is particularly powerful. "Static" here means done before any execution is attempted, whereas "dynamic" means done at execution time; "typing" means the verification of consistency, whereas "binding" means the association of a feature name (such as *redeem*) with an actual feature, such as the redeeming operation for ticket awards. The verification is done as early as possible, prior to execution; but the binding is done as late as possible, during execution. Static typing means a static guarantee that **at least one feature** will be applicable; dynamic binding means that in all execution-time cases **the right feature** will be applied.

Not all O-O languages are statically typed. The most famous example of a dynamically typed language is Smalltalk, where the preceding discussion does not hold: type declarations are not required, so that a wrongly used feature will produce a run-time error — "*message not understood*" — usually causing the application to terminate abnormally. Although perhaps defensible for research or experimentation software, dynamic typing has always struck me as unacceptable for production systems; bugs should be fixed by the software team at the time of development, not passed on to end-users of the product (such as Frequent Flyer program personnel). Many studies have confirmed what every software manager knows intuitively: the later an error is detected, the more costly it will be to fix; and the cost grows exponentially. Static typing is a way to catch bugs before they have the time to catch you.

CONCEPT TEN: AUTOMATIC MEMORY MANAGEMENT

> **MEMORY MANAGEMENT PRINCIPLE**
>
> An object-oriented environment should automatically take care of reclaiming the memory used by objects that are not accessible any more to the execution of a system.

For this last concept on our list we are entering the area of implementation support for object-oriented development. But the memory management mechanism is not a little internal detail; it is a key part of the supporting technology, which makes the more highbrow stuff possible. Some presentations of object technology, especially those which focus on analysis, sneer as such lowly details, or ignore them totally. This is about as useful as describing the operation of a car and concentrating solely on the external components — steering wheel and pedals — and forgetting to mention that none of this would be very useful without an engine and gas.

The execution of an object-oriented system tends to create many objects; some of these objects will eventually become unreachable from the active ones and hence useless. Good implementations of object-oriented languages address this problem by providing an automatic memory management mechanism, or **garbage collector**, that periodically looks for unreachable objects and reclaims their memory. Without this facility it is difficult to write realistic O-O applications.

Modern garbage collectors can make themselves quite unobtrusive: they are triggered only once in a while, and do not interrupt the application for perceptible amounts of time. Without them, developers would have to devote a large part of their efforts to cleaning up their memory usage. Not only is this manual memory management tedious; it is also error-prone, as the software can all too easily free an object even though some remote part of the application still has a reference to it. This can cause some horrendous bugs — all the more difficult to track that the cause of the error is often far removed from its intermittent manifestation.

One may compare the role of automatic garbage collection in O-O development to that of automatic register allocation in normal high-level programming. Once upon a time, programmers had to devote considerable effort to allocating the machine's registers to the variables of their programs. With the advent of high-level languages and compilers, this burden was removed from programmers so that they could use their astuteness to solve problems more directly relevant to their customers. Garbage collection is one more step in this continual effort to free developers' energy for truly constructive goals.

SEAMLESSNESS

Where do the Ten Key Concepts just seen belong? Are they "programming" notions, in the restricted sense of the term (implementation)? Do they affect the design level? Or can they be applied to analysis, that is to say to the abstract study of a system's requirements?

The answer: all of the above. The same ideas will permeate the entire software construction process. It would be a mistake, in particular, to understand them as implementation techniques only. The client and inheritance relations, governed by contracts, can exist between analysis classes describing models of objects from external physical systems, such as a class *MEMBER* in a Frequent Flyer system; between design classes describing software architecture decisions, for example a class *SESSION* in an interactive text processing system; and between implementation classes describing choices of data structures and algorithms, such as a class *LINKED_LIST*.

> One exception: the last principle, Memory Management, addresses an implementation issue, although as noted that issue is essential to make the other aspects of the technology possible.

Seamlessness means more than just being able to use similar ideas at various levels. Object technology reduces the traditional differences between analysis, design and implementation. Instead of rigidly separated phases the method promotes a continuous view of software development where the various activities follow each other seamlessly.

This property is one of the principal innovations of object technology. It is one of the concepts that a manager in charge of supervising the introduction of O-O development must understand, since in addition to its technical consequences it has a considerable effect on the software process, on team organization, and on the definition of jobs.

These aspects will be explored in the rest of this book, especially in the study of the object-oriented lifecycle in the following chapter; see in particular "SEAMLESSNESS", page 48. They can be summarized by a simple principle:

SEAMLESSNESS PRINCIPLE

Object-oriented ideas are meant to be applied to all steps of software development, including analysis, design, implementation and maintenance, and to decrease the gaps between these steps.

OBJECT-ORIENTED LANGUAGES

To implement an object-oriented design, you will need an object-oriented language. (It is in principle possible to translate the design to a traditional language, but this means doing the work of an O-O language compiler yourself, not a very attractive idea. See the "Seriousness Principle", page 76.) Let us briefly review the major offerings in this area. I have been actively involved with one of them (Eiffel) and hence cannot claim to be an unopinionated observer, but this does not preclude giving an overview of the major features of each approach.

Object-oriented languages, and the whole O-O field, got their start in the nineteen-sixties with the publication in 1967 of Simula, a simulation language that was also a general-purpose O-O language. It is impressive to see how many of the basic ideas were there. In the past ten years a number of O-O languages have appeared; three of them have attracted the most attention:

- Smalltalk.
- C++.
- Eiffel.

Smalltalk, whose first versions predated those of the other two, was instrumental in making object-oriented ideas appealing to a large audience through the quality of its user interface. The language has been widely used for experimentation and prototyping (see the discussion of this term in chapter 4). But its lack of static typing, assertions and multiple inheritance make its use dubious for production-grade software. Typing in particular is an issue: as noted above, it is not safe, in serious, mission-critical applications, to have to wait until run time to find out whether a feature is applicable to an object, and see the application crash if one infrequent case has been forgotten. Smalltalk has also been criticized for the performance of the code that its implementations generate. It does, however, provide an attractive introduction to object-orientation through the power of its environment, and in the nineteen-eighties succeeded magnificently at a task that Simula had failed to achieve: making object-oriented ideas visible and attractive to a large community.

C++ is the result of extending the C language with a number of O-O constructs. It is particularly attractive to companies that have a major investment in C and hope for a smooth transition to object-oriented development. The C heritage also makes it difficult to obtain the full benefits of the method; garbage collection, for example, is usually not supported in C++, and the type system is hybrid, mixing C concepts with those of object technology and preventing a full application of static typing principles. C++ has recently come under intense criticism for its complexity; the C++ extract on page 26, which deals with manual implementation of memory management facilities, is typical of the difficulty of reading C++ code, due in particular to the use of many low-level, machine-oriented constructs inherited from C, such as * (giving the content of a memory address) and & (giving the address of a variable), of which it is easy to include an occurrence too few or too many. But C++ may be credited for having brought object-oriented concepts to the masses; it is a transition technology that has been helpful to many people with a C background.

Eiffel, whose syntax is used in the examples of the Appendix, is an attempt to keep the advantages of both of the previous approaches without their limitations. From C++ it retains the ability to produce highly efficient code, whose performance is comparable to that of programs written in such traditional languages as C and Fortran, and to interface easily with existing code (all current Eiffel compilers generate C output). Like Smalltalk it uses a "pure-O-O" approach uncompromised by hybridization with non-O-O languages. Among the innovations of Eiffel are assertions, a carefully designed view of inheritance (in particular to address multiple inheritance), and a strict approach to static typing. Eiffel has been widely used in applications with high reliability and efficiency requirements, such as telecommunications, CAD-CAM, banking (in particular the challenging area of options and derivatives trading). It is also popular with universities for teaching programming and other software topics at all levels. The following extract, taken from a later discussion of the use of object-oriented notations for analysis, is typical of the look and feel of Eiffel texts. It is extracted from a specification of the notion of vat for a chemical plant; the *require*, *ensure* and *invariant* clauses are assertions, expressing the contracts.

```
deferred class VAT inherit

    TANK

feature

    fill is
                -- Fill the vat.
        require
            in_valve.open; out_valve.closed
        deferred
        ensure
            in_valve.closed; out_valve.closed; is_full
        end;

    [Other features: is_full, is_empty, empty, in_valve, out_valve,
    gauge, maximum ...]

invariant

    is_full = (gauge >= .97 * maximum) and (gauge <= 1.03 * maximum)
end
```

AN EIFFEL EXTRACT

(For details on the example see page 181.)

```
// These classes implement the necessary logic          RPtr& operator=(Counted *tp)
// for building reference counted objects                  { if (ptr) ptr–>delref();
// and the associated pointers.                              ptr = tp;
                                                            if(ptr) ptr–>addref();
class counted {                                             return *this
    friend class Rptr;                                    }
                                                    } ;
    int nreferences;
        // number of references to this object
                                                    #define RPtr (T) name2 (Rptr_,T)
    addRef ()
        { nreferences++; }                          #defineMakeRPtr (T)

    delRef ()
        {                                           class RPtr (t) : public RPtr_base {
            if (--nreferences)                          Counted *ptr;
                delete this;                        public:
        }                                               RPtr(T) ()
public:                                                     : RPtr_base()
    Counted ()                                              { }
        { nreferences = 0; }
    ~Counted();                                         RPtr(T) (RPtr(T)& r)
} ;                                                         : RPtr_base(r)
                                                            { }
Class RPtr_base {
  protected:                                            RPtr(T) (T *tp)
    Counted *ptr;                                           : RPtr_base ((Counted *) T)
    RPtr_base()                                             { }
        { ptr = 0; ]
                                                        ~RPtr (T) ()
    RPtr(RPtr& r)                                           { }
        { ptr = r.ptr;
          if(ptr) ptr–>addref();                      RPtr(T)& operator=(RPtr(T)& r)
          return *this;                                   { *((RPtr_base *) this) = r; }
        }
                                                        RPtr(T)& operator=(T *tp)
    RPtr(Counted *tp)                                       { *((RPtr_base *) this) =
        { ptr = tp;                                           (Counted *) tp; }
          if(ptr) ptr–>addref();
          return *this;                               T& operator *()
        }                                                 { assert(ptr); return *((T *) ptr); }

    ~RPtr()                                             operator T *()
        { if (ptr)  ptr–>delref(); }                      { return (T *) ptr; }

    RPtr& operator=(RPtr& r)                            int operator !()
        { if (ptr) ptr–delref();                          { return !ptr; }
          ptr = r.ptr;                              };
          if(ptr) ptr–>addref();
          return *this
        }
```

A C++ EXTRACT

(From: J. S. Shapiro, *A C++ Toolkit*, Prentice Hall, 1991, pp. 222-223; reprinted with permission.)

IMPLEMENTATION ASPECTS

To use an object-oriented language you will need the appropriate tools. O-O languages are either directly interpreted or compiled into machine code.

An increasingly popular approach is to use a compiler that instead of directly generating machine code uses C as an intermediate language: the O-O compiler generates C output and relies on a C compiler to obtain an executable result. This technique is used by many C++ compilers and all current Eiffel compilers. It presents a number of advantages:

- C is a sort of universal assembly language, implementations of which are available on most platforms. This facilitates portability.

- The use of C as implementation vehicle also facilitates interfacing O-O applications with existing software, for example graphics or database tools, many of which use C.

- C compilers are adept at handling many optimizations.

Once compiled, whether into C or something else, an object-oriented application will need a set of facilities for memory allocation, garbage collection, signal handling and interfacing with the operating system. Providing these facilities is the task of the **run-time system,** which must be linked with the application to permit its execution.

OBJECT-ORIENTED ENVIRONMENTS

The object-oriented paradigm provides a number of ideas that can be fruitfully applied to development environments, as was first brilliantly illustrated by Smalltalk.

A word of caution here: the marketing appeal of the word "object-oriented" has led to its over-use and devaluation, almost to the point of absurdity; some tools, it would seem, base their claims to object orientation on having gained a few icons and pull-down menus. But in fact the notion of object-oriented environment is a serious one, resulting from applying O-O ideas to the interaction between software developers and their tools.

To help you get a feel for these concepts here are a few examples from a recent development in the field, the ISE Eiffel environment (running on Windows, Unix, VMS etc.).

Where traditional environments have **function**-based tools — a compiler, a debugger, a pretty-printer, a CASE (Computer-Aided Software Engineering) program generator and so on — an object-oriented environment will have tools based on **data abstractions**: a class tool, a feature tool, a system tool, a project tool. Each one of these tools is based on one of the data abstractions of interest to developers: classes, features, systems, projects.

The screen shot at the top of the following page shows a class tool. The tool has been *targeted* to a particular class, *STRING* (a library class). It shows an extract of the class text, written in Eiffel. (This figure and the ones that follow it are reprinted courtesy of ISE.)

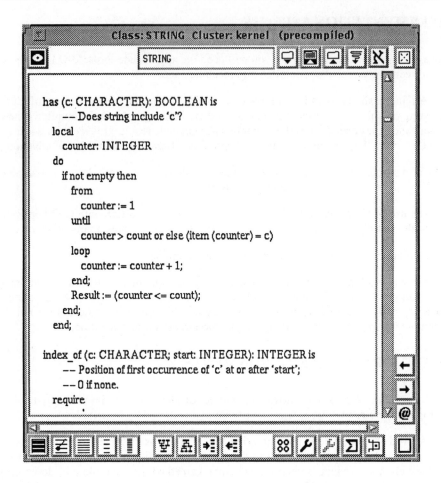

```
Class: STRING  Cluster: kernel  (precompiled)

                    STRING

has (c: CHARACTER): BOOLEAN is
    -- Does string include 'c'?
  local
    counter: INTEGER
  do
    if not empty then
      from
        counter := 1
      until
        counter > count or else (item (counter) = c)
      loop
        counter := counter + 1;
      end;
      Result := (counter <= count);
    end;
  end;

index_of (c: CHARACTER; start: INTEGER): INTEGER is
    -- Position of first occurrence of 'c' at or after 'start';
    -- 0 if none.
  require
```

A CLASS TOOL IN TEXT FORMAT

Various formats are applicable to the class, represented by the bottom row of icons. For example the icon labeled ▤ represents the short form (the basic interface documentation for a class, see page 169); the icon labeled ▼ represents the ancestors — the inheritance structure that leads to the class.

Two of the available formats are shown on the adjacent page:

• If you click on the Ancestors format icon ▼ the tool will switch to a format that shows the ancestor inheritance structure:

• Or you can click on the Routines format 🔧 to obtain a list of some of the features of the class, each with the indication of the class from which it comes in the inheritance hierarchy.

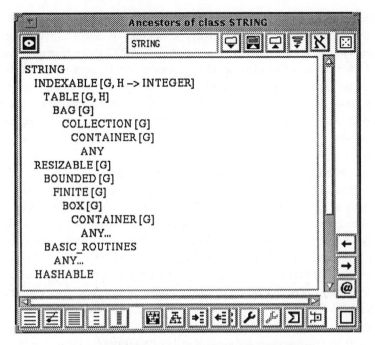

A CLASS TOOL IN ANCESTORS FORMAT

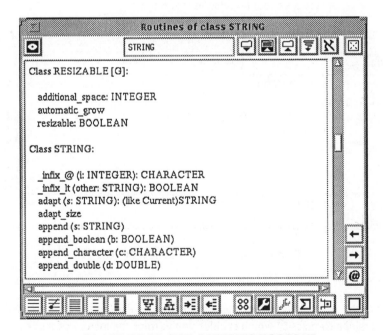

A CLASS TOOL IN ROUTINES FORMAT

The transposition of O-O development concepts to the environment itself is clear: in the same way that a typical O-O operation applies an operation to a target object, here each tool is targeted to a development object — the class *STRING* in the example. Similarly, the formats at the bottom of the window are the equivalent of the **query** features (see page 158) applicable to the instances of a class; they make it possible to obtain various kinds of information about the class. There are also **commands,** which can change the status; for example the Project tool will have a Compile button to perform a quick recompilation of the current project.

It is also interesting to see how such an object-oriented environment addresses the browsing problem. Developers will often need to explore the structure of an O-O system, to find relatives of a class (heirs, parents, clients, suppliers) and properties of its features. Older environments provided a tool, the *browser,* to perform that task. But, like a subroutine in traditional software decomposition, a browser is a function-oriented tool. Instead, we can use the object-oriented facilities outlined above to provide browsing without a browser. Under the formats shown, everything is **clickable:** you can mouse-click on the name of any class, feature or other developer object, and drag-and-drop it to the appropriate tool to find out more information. For example, looking at the first few lines of the last figure, you can click on the name of any one of the classes *RESIZABLE, INTEGER, BOOLEAN* and so on, and drag-and-drop it either to a different class tool or to the given class tool (so as to *retarget* it to the given class). You can also click on a feature such as *resizable* to bring up a feature tool targeted to that feature:

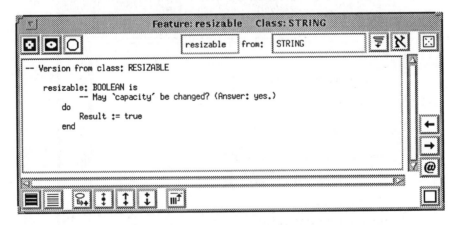

A FEATURE TOOL IN TEXT FORMAT

Among the format buttons in the bottom row of the feature tool you will find the Ancestor Versions format ⬍ which enables you to trace the history of the feature through the inheritance hierarchy:

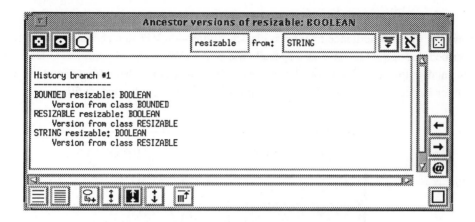

A FEATURE TOOL IN ANCESTORS VERSION FORMAT

Here as elsewhere all the class and feature names are clickable. This provides a powerful hypertext-like mechanism for exploring the various developer objects and the many transmutations to which they are subjected in the object-oriented software development process.

The key to the flexibility and ease of use of these mechanisms is the way they apply O-O principles not just to the software being developed, but also to the process of producing it interactively. The facilities that have just been sketched are only a basic subset; the environment provides many further mechanisms, all fitting in the same framework, for such activities as compiling, interactive debugging and others. A high-level analysis and design tool (EiffelCase) provides the equivalent for the earliest stages of software construction.

OBJECT-ORIENTED ANALYSIS

An application of object technology has attracted much attention in the past few years: object-oriented analysis, which uses concepts of data abstraction and inheritance to model problems before (or without) attempting to build software solutions.

The object-oriented method is attractive here because of its modeling power. Kristen Nygaard, one of the designers of Simula, coined the aphorism *to program is to understand.* A consequence is that many of the O-O mechanisms initially devised (by Nygaard and others) to facilitate programming also facilitate understanding and hence modeling, even if the process stops there rather than continuing with the programming of a software system.

A number of methods have been devised to take advantage of this strength of object-oriented ideas; the bibliography lists some of them. In many cases, however, you do not need much more than what has already been introduced in this chapter. Combining the ideas of data abstraction, classes, information hiding, client-supplier relationships, classification through inheritance and contracts yields a powerful method for modeling external systems, long before thinking about any design or implementation decision.

The Eiffel example given on page 25 provides a good example of this approach. It shows the use of inheritance to express classifications — a *VAT* in a chemical plant being described through inheritance as a special case of a *TANK* — and of contracts to state the input and output conditions on the corresponding operations; here for example is the contract for the operation that fills a vat, represented in the class by feature *fill*:

fill	**OBLIGATIONS**	**BENEFITS**
Client	*(Satisfy precondition:)* Input valve must be open, and output valve closed.	*(From postcondition:)* Get the vat in a state in which it is full, with the valves in the proper positions.
Supplier	*(Satisfy postcondition:)* Fill vat and leave the valves in the proper positions.	*(From precondition:)* No need to worry about initial cases in which input valve is closed or output valve open.

People trained in conventional approaches, for whom "analysis" connotes imprecise descriptions relying on the infamous "bubbles and arrows" of Structured Analysis and similar methods, might react to the class text of page 25 by crying: "This is a program text, not analysis!". Such a reaction, however, is unfounded. Nothing in that extract has anything to do with implementation. The extract would be easy to explain to someone who went to high school around 1930, but lived with an Amazonian tribe ever since and never heard about computers, let alone software — but knows about chemical plants and vats. It is a pure conceptual description.

To make these techniques attractive to a wide range of users it is often desirable to provide other representations as well. This is where the bubbles and arrows come back: graphical views of object-oriented analysis models, deduced from specifications such as the one for *VAT*, can be helpful to support discussions with customers and prospective users. The following screen shot shows an example of such a graphical system description, produced by the EiffelCase tool in the ISE Eiffel environment.

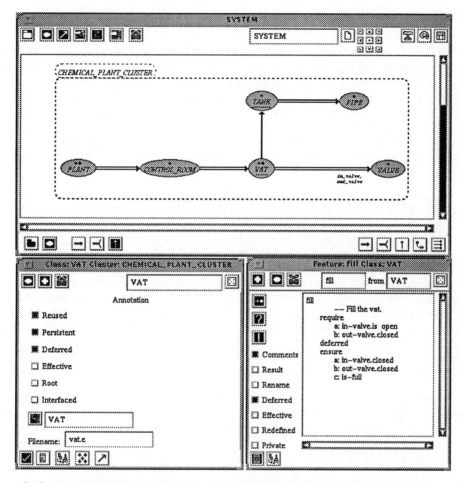

O-O ANALYSIS CASE TOOLS: A SYSTEM STRUCTURE DIAGRAM
(with feature and class tools)
EiffelCase output; reproduced by permission of ISE.

Even then the formal version (such as the text of page 25) should serve as the reference of last resort if you need to answer precise questions about the specification, such as "is a vat considered full if its gauge shows 96.5%?". Graphical descriptions are widely and properly praised for their expressiveness, but they are not the appropriate tool when precision is the goal. In such cases, essential to the quality of the eventual system, you need formal text. So if both a graphical and a textual versions of the object-oriented model are available, two-way tools should be available to enable the seamless translation of graphical input into a text form and, conversely, the production of graphics from text. Support for the first direction is common in CASE tools; the reverse facility is more challenging and has only recently become available, in products such as EiffelCase.

THE NEW ROLE OF ANALYSIS

Object technology does not just affect *how* to do analysis, but also the very nature of the analysis process, although this point seems to have been missed by much of the current O-O analysis literature. Conventional views of the software process, such as the waterfall model discussed in the next chapter, rely on the assumption, explicit or not, that the initial statement of user requirements is sacred. Software developers are not supposed to discuss the requirements; they are supposed to implement them! Object technology's emphasis on reusability, however, changes this outlook; it becomes *permitted*, even encouraged, to come up with alternative suggestions in response to a requirements document:

> **THE FIRST PRINCIPLE OF OBJECT-ORIENTED ANALYSIS**
>
> It is all right to talk back to customers.

Assume that you are in charge of software developments in a company, and that by using O-O techniques you have been able, over the past months or years, to produce a pool of reusable components. You may have been officially asked to do this; or, more commonly, you may have acquired components from outside sources, and quietly growing some of your own components out of actual developments done in response to earlier customer requests, using techniques of *generalization* described in a later chapter (see "THE MÉTHODE CHAMPENOISE", page 119).

Whatever the case, you now have these components at your disposal. Then if a new customer request comes in (whether from an in-house user or from the outside), possibly complex and over-ambitious, you may be able to reply with a counter-proposal: a suggestion for a solution that, although slightly different from the customer's requirements as initially stated, may be built by reusing, adapting and complementing existing components, much faster and possibly at a fraction of the cost of implementing the original idea.

What matters in the end, of course, is customer satisfaction; only the customers will decide what is acceptable and what is not. They may well reject your suggestion as being too far from what they need. Such a reaction does not mean, however, that you are back to business as usual; it means the start of a negotiation. Their original request may have been too baroque; your original response may have been too simplistic; you should talk. After a few rounds of proposals and counter-proposals you may reach an acceptable middle ground — a specification that is powerful enough to meet their needs, and realistic enough to enable effective development based at least in part on the reusable components and tools that you have already accumulated. To summarize:

> **THE SECOND PRINCIPLE OF OBJECT-ORIENTED ANALYSIS**
>
> In a corporate environment that fosters object-orientation and reuse, analysis becomes a negotiation process.

If you consider the practice of software development, this idea is not really new: whatever the theory may have been in traditional software engineering textbooks and official company policies, some kind of haggling has always been necessary to reconcile the desirable with the doable. Object technology goes further by making this process official and associating it with reuse. This is but one area where the technology does not just give us better tools to tackle the traditional problems of software engineering, but partly changes the problems themselves.

It is striking to see, once again, how the object-oriented method brings to software development the techniques, practices and thought patterns of business life. Negotiation, like many others concepts encountered in this chapter — contracts, centralization versus decentralization, the need to delegate tasks, the separation between a strategy and its implementation — is typical of these ideas, familiar to a business person, which with object technology find a clear and fruitful application to the technical problem of developing software for quality and productivity.

OBJECT-ORIENTED DATABASES

Another area that has been influenced by O-O ideas is databases.

Until then, aside from a few strongholds of hierarchical approaches (IMS in the IBM mainframe world) and network models, the undisputed victor was the relational model, which established its dominance in the nineteen-eighties. Relational databases hold data in the form of tables of records. Each record is made of a number of fields; the field types are the same for all records in a table. The join operation makes it possible to combine data from two tables, yielding another table; the projection operation makes it possible to select a subset of the field types of a table, yielding a simpler table.

Relational databases have been particularly effective for applications that manipulate possibly large quantities of data with a relatively simple structure. The reason why the structure must remain simple is that the relational model does not support, in the normalized" form, records whose fields may be references to other records. It is possible to emulate references by introducing, for each type of object that may be the target of a reference, a field type containing an integer or some other key that uniquely identifies each record, and relying on joins and projections. But this is clumsy for anything beyond the simplest reference structures.

Object-oriented databases use a more advanced data model, based on some of the ideas described in this chapter, in particular abstraction and inheritance, and on the concept of object identification (each object in the database is assigned a unique identifier).

Not surprisingly, O-O databases were first used in areas such as Computer Aided Design which require sophisticated modeling techniques. In the model for the design of a new product, say a car, a large number of components will be connected through numerous dependencies: the car has many parts, such as its engine; each part may have further components, such as an engine's carburetor; a component has an associated deadline, budget and person in charge; the person in charge is an employee that has a rank, salary and supervisor; and so on. Relational databases do not offer such flexibility.

Object-oriented databases are now spreading to other application areas such as banking and finance. It is fair to note, however, that even though the technology is progressing fast it has not yet reached the level of refinement of either its counterparts in the software development world (O-O languages, tools and environments) or its predecessors in the database world (relational databases with their mechanisms for concurrency, integrity control, rollback etc.).

For companies that have large data needs and are going into object-oriented software development, the question then arises of what data model to use. The answer depends on the context:

- If you are manipulating data with a relatively simple structure, or data created and still accessed by relational tools, you may be better off with a library that provides an interface between an object-oriented environment and a relational database. A number of such libraries are available, some for C++, some for Eiffel, some for Smalltalk; ISE's EiffelStore, for example, currently supports Oracle and Sybase. The natural mapping is to associate a relational record with an object, and a table with a class.

- If, however, your data structure is more complex, and you can define it as you please — that is to say, you are not tied to a mass of pre-existing relational data — then an object-oriented database, or the persistence mechanism of your object-oriented language (such as Eiffel's *STORABLE* facility), may be the way to go.

A number of companies have recently introduced a solution that attempts to yield the best of both worlds: hybrid databases, which retain a number of relational mechanisms while adding object-oriented concepts.

NETWORKS AND OBJECT REQUEST BROKERS

A final aspect of the technology deserves to be mentioned. With the growth of networks and distributed computing, the industry has increasingly been looking for simple ways of exchanging structured data between different processes. The abstraction mechanisms of object-oriented programming can help.

Environments such as Apple's Macintosh have addressed a simple form of this goal of application interoperability by providing standardized formats that allow various applications to use common data; the standard example is a word processor integrating data from a spreadsheet. But much more is needed. At the other extreme you find the Unix operating system, where the only generally accepted standard is text, forcing every application to define its own communication formats — so that, not surprisingly, little or no communication is by default possible between tools originating from different suppliers.

Object technology appears promising here because of its emphasis on abstraction: to enable an effective form of interaction between applications, whether they reside on the same machine or run on different processors, communicating through abstract class interfaces is preferable to techniques that would be based on lower-level standards such as text formats. This is the idea behind object request brokers.

At the time of writing two standardization efforts have attracted attention: Microsoft's OLE (Object Linking and Embedding) and a proposal called CORBA (Common Object Request Broker Architecture), whose CORBA 1 version is not platform-independent while the CORBA 2 version, which promises interoperability between platforms, is still under discussion. Related efforts include the OpenDoc multi-document architecture, driven by a group of hardware and software companies.

All this evokes the famous comment that "standards are great — that's why there are so many of them". One can hope the situation will stabilize, enabling object technology to provide another key benefit to the computer industry.

BIBLIOGRAPHY

[The books marked with an asterisk * in this bibliography and those of subsequent chapters are part of Prentice Hall's Object-Oriented Series, to which this book also belongs.]

A general introduction to object-oriented concepts may be found in my *Object-Oriented Software Construction** (Prentice Hall, 1988, revised edition to appear in 1995), which discusses the intellectual background for the method, and presents O-O techniques in light of the software quality factors listed in the present chapter. If you prefer smaller volumes, see *A Book of Object-Oriented Knowledge** by Brian Henderson-Sellers (Prentice Hall, 1991), notable for its full-page viewgraphs which readers are invited to reproduce for talks introducing O-O concepts to their companies. Other introductions include *Object-Oriented Methods* by Ian Graham (Addison-Wesley, second edition, 1994), whose coverage is particularly broad.

Two books are, like the present one, specifically targeted towards managers rather than software developers: David Taylor's *Object-Oriented Technology: A Manager's Guide* (Addison-Wesley, 1992) and Ivar Jacobson's *The Object Advantage: Business Process Reengineering with Object Technology* (Addison-Wesley, 1994).

The concept of Design by Contract is discussed in *Object-Oriented Software Construction* and also in the article *Applying "Design by Contract"*, in *Computer (IEEE)*, 25, 10, pages 40-51, October 1992.

The principles of designing libraries are explored in my book *Reusable Software: The Base Object-Oriented Component Libraries** (Prentice Hall, 1994), which introduces a general-purpose taxonomy of the fundamental structures of computing. The environment illustrated in this chapter and its design principles are presented in *An Object-Oriented Environment: Principles and Application** (Prentice Hall, 1994).

Here are the basic references on the object-oriented languages mentioned in this chapter: on Smalltalk, *Smalltalk-80: The Language and its Implementation* by Adele Goldberg and David Robson (Addison-Wesley, 1983); on C++, *The C++ Programming Language* by Bjarne Stroustrup (Addison-Wesley, second edition, 1993); on Eiffel, *Eiffel: The Language** (Prentice Hall, 1992). The Objective-C language, another O-O extension of C, is described in *Object-Oriented Programming: An Evolutionary Approach, Second edition* by Brad J. Cox and Andrew J. Novobilski, Addison-Wesley, 1990.

Several introductory books are available on object-oriented databases. See for example Won Kim's *Introduction to Object-Oriented Databases*, MIT Press, 1990. Techniques for combining object-oriented development with a relational database management system are studied in the book by Waldén and Nerson cited next.

On O-O analysis there is also an abundant literature. Closest to the view presented in this chapter is the BON method (Business Object Notation), a "second-generation" analysis and design method described in *Seamless Object-Oriented Software Architecture: Design and Analysis of Reliable Systems** by Kim Waldén and Jean-Marc Nerson, Prentice Hall, 1995.

Among earlier texts on analysis one of the most popular is Ivar Jacobson's *Object-Oriented Software Engineering: A Use Case Driven Approach*, Addison-Wesley, 1992, introducing the notion of "use cases" as a way to detect scenarios that will help define the final architecture. Also widely used is *Object-Oriented Modeling and Design* by James Rumbaugh, Michael Blaha, William Premerlani, Frederick Eddy and William Lorensen (all then of General Electric), Prentice Hall, 1991, introducing the OMT method which combines O-O concepts with ideas from entity-relationship modeling. Yet another influential book is *Designing Object-Oriented Software* by Rebecca Wirfs-Brock, Brian Wilkerson and Laura Wiener, Prentice Hall, 1990.

Other notable contributions include the MOSES method, presented in *BOOKTWO of Object-Oriented Knowledge: The Working Object** by Brian Henderson-Sellers and Julian Edwards, Prentice Hall, 1994, which also contains a survey of the field; the work of Haim Kilov and James Ross, presented in their *Information Modeling: An Object-Oriented Approach**, Prentice Hall, 1994, establishing a link with information modeling and relying on the notion of contract; and Hewlett-Packard's Fusion method, introduced in *Object-Oriented Development: The Fusion Method** by Derek Coleman et al., Prentice Hall, 1994, which relates the analysis task to the subsequent phases of software development. See also *Designing Object Systems** by Steve Cook and John Daniels, Prentice Hall, 1994, describing the Syntropy method.

Additional analysis books include *Object Lifecycles: Modeling the World in States* by Sally Shlaer and Steve Mellor (Prentice Hall, 1992); *Object-Oriented Analysis* by Peter Coad and Edward Yourdon (Prentice Hall, 1990); *Object-Oriented Analysis and Design with Applications* by Grady Booch (Addison-Wesley, 1994); and *Object-Oriented Analysis and Design* by James Martin and James J. Odell, Prentice Hall, 1992. As the concentration of publication dates indicates, this is a very active field.

3

The object-oriented lifecycle

Object technology affects the very organization of software development. In particular, it puts into question the traditional models of the software lifecycle, whether theoretical or actually applied.

Let us examine these traditional models and then see how O-O development leads to a new approach, the *cluster* model, which retains the advantages of the earlier models while allowing object technology to reach its full bloom.

WHAT USE FOR LIFECYCLE MODELS?

First it is useful to reflect on the role of models. If you look up the word *model* in a dictionary, you will find two separate meanings:

- A model can be, especially in science, an abstracted version of reality, as in "The relativistic model of space and time explains phenomena that do not fit the Newtonian model". This is the meaning of *model* that the Oxford English Dictionary gives as "a summary, epitome or abstract".

- Or it can be an ideal, often far ahead of the reality, as in "She is a model for all of us to follow". The OED calls this "a perfect exemplar of some excellence".

A model is descriptive in the first case, prescriptive in the second. One thinks of La Bruyère's famous characterization of the two great dramatists of the seventeenth century, both of whom can be said to present models of humanity in their plays: *Racine paints men as they are, Corneille as they should be.*

Lifecycle models, which sprang into existence in the early nineteen-seventies, have been used in both descriptive and prescriptive roles. This will also be true of the replacement presented later in this chapter.

One should not attach too much value to such models. Producing software is neither cooking nor alcoholism recovery; no 12-step program can be expected to guarantee success. But if applied with reason models are a precious management tool. In their prescriptive role they enable the project manager to ensure an orderly process and to plan activities, resource allocations and personnel assignments. In their descriptive role, they help assess progress and detect a delay before it becomes a crisis.

THE WATERFALL MODEL

The obligatory starting point for discussions of lifecycle model is the so-called waterfall model, first proposed by W. W. Royce from the US Air Force in a 1970 paper and popularized among others by the articles and book of B.W. Boehm, then at TRW. Although many variants of this model exist, they all more or less resemble the general scheme shown on the facing page.

The waterfall divides the software construction process into a number of successive steps. In the variant shown by the figure, the role of these steps is as follows:

- The feasibility study explores whether or not to build a software system. Obviously the following steps will only take place if the resulting decision is positive.

- Requirements analysis determines what functions the system must satisfy.

- Specification yields a more precise and formal version of the requirements; the results of the previous steps are meant to be understandable by customers (future users), whereas the specification is intended for software people.

- Global design defines the architecture of the system: its division into modules and the overall organization of its data structures.

- Detailed design yields a precise description of each module and data structure.

- Implementation produces the actual software text and data structures.

- Validation & Verification (often called V&V for short) checks the adequacy of what has been developed. The traditional distinction is that validation assesses whether the system addresses the requirements ("is it the right system?") whereas verification assesses internal consistency ("is the system right?").

- Distribution gets the software to its users.

The exact division into steps may vary, but one principle always applies: the development team is not supposed to start a step before the preceding step has been completed, its results validated, and the corresponding documents accepted. For example you should not embark on the design phases until the specification has been successfully finished.

The waterfall model also includes a rule (suggested by the up and down arrows that give the model its distinctive graphical appearance and its name) that any changes to already approved results must be limited to the immediately preceding step.

IN FAVOR OF THE WATERFALL

Although it will soon be clear that the waterfall model is not adapted to modern software development, it is important to realize that not everything is wrong with it.

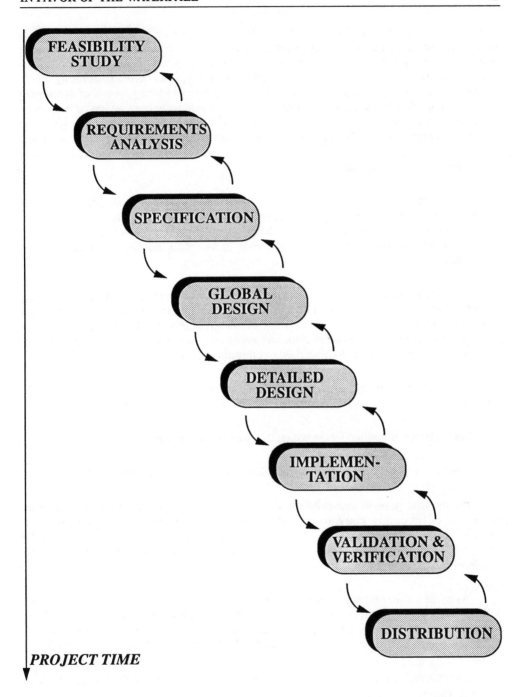

SOFTWARE LIFECYCLE: THE WATERFALL MODEL

First one should keep in mind when and why the waterfall model was introduced. It was a reaction against an all too prevalent model, or non-model, of software development: what can be called the *code it now, fix it later* approach, where programmers do not use any systematic organization but go to implementation right away without devoting much attention to analysis or design; this almost inevitably leads to many rounds of debugging and rewriting. (A note for the younger members of our audience: here we are talking about software practices of a time long past. Of course nothing of the sort can be observed in today's software world.) The contribution of the waterfall model was to carry loud and clear the message that software development is serious business and must follow professional engineering practices.

In particular the model has introduced two sound ideas, which we must retain: the emphasis on upstream activities (analysis, specification, design), favoring abstraction and avoiding too much early preoccupation with implementation details; and the inclusion of a separate Validation and Verification step, meant to ascertain that the software meets its objectives.

Perhaps paradoxically, another contribution of the waterfall is what it does *not* include. The model implicitly indicates that some software development activities, important though they may be, should not be handled as separate lifecycle steps. For example there is no documentation step; this suggests — correctly — that we should treat documentation as an activity to be carried out throughout the lifecycle.

Finally, the following arguments in favor of the waterfall model (made by B.W. Boehm in his book *Software Engineering Economics*) are worth considering:

• The activities identified by the waterfall's steps are necessary.

• The order in which the waterfall schedules these activities is the right one.

On the first point it seems hardly debatable that any non-trivial project will need some kind of feasibility study, some analysis, some design and so on. One qualification, though: in O-O development the middle steps, design and implementation, tend to be collapsed into just one step. More on this later; but with this reservation we may consider that Boehm's first argument essentially holds.

As to the second argument, what better order could we find than the waterfall's? Few software engineering professors would teach that the ideal sequence of events is to implement, then distribute, then design, then validate, then do the analysis if any time is left (even if such an ordering is not unheard of in the history of real software projects).

So if the activities are essentially appropriate and so is their order, what can be wrong with the waterfall model?

As will turn out, quite a few things.

THE DOWNSIDE OF THE WATERFALL

The first major problem with the waterfall model is its lack of support for requirements change. The model implicitly assumes that at the end of the second phase (requirements analysis) the requirements are frozen; all that remains is to refine and implement them. Such an assumption only has a remote connection with the reality of software development. It would be a remarkable project indeed — worth reporting to the press — that would not experience any requirements change. In practice, as you start designing and implementing the system, as you start putting early versions in the hands of users, you get better ideas as to what it should be doing. To avoid anarchy, this process of frequent change should be carefully managed and controlled; but denying or ignoring change does not help.

The second limitation is the model's lack of support for software maintenance (defined as whatever comes after the first official release of a product). True, some variants of the model, such as the one in Boehm's book, include a last step labeled "operations and maintenance". But this looks like lip service: whereas all of the previous steps denote different activities, going into maintenance mode means doing more of the same — more analysis, more design, more implementation, more V & V. Since a number of studies of where the money goes in software construction suggest that 50% to 80% of software costs are spent on maintenance activities rather than upfront development, we may expect more help from the lifecycle model in understanding and controlling this activity.

Also dangerous is the highly synchronous nature of the waterfall process: like the regiments in an 18th-century army, the various parts of a project must all march at the same speed, since the model prescribes specifying the whole system, then designing the whole system, and so on. Effective software management is more like guerrilla warfare: to do a proper job, the manager needs mechanisms for quick dynamic reconfiguration in case some part of the project is delayed, or proceeds faster than expected. This point will deserve further attention (see "RISK MANAGEMENT AND DYNAMIC RECONFIGURATION", page 57).

The fourth deficiency, perhaps the most obviously damaging, is the tardy appearance of the main product of software development: software — or, to use a more mundane term, code. Although the software lifecycle also has other products (analysis documents, design reports, user documentation, operating procedures, database schemata...), what really counts in the end, what will bring profit if the project succeeds and layoffs if it fails, is code. Code is to our industry what bread is to a baker and books to a writer. But with the waterfall code only appears late in the process; for a manager this is an unacceptable risk factor. Anyone with practical experience in software development knows how many things can go wrong once you get down to code: a brilliant design idea whose implementation turns out to require tens of megabytes of space or minutes of response time; beautiful bubbles and arrows that cannot be implemented; an operating system update, crucial to the project, which comes five weeks late; an obscure bug that takes ages to be fixed. Unless you start coding early in the process, you will not be able to control your project.

THE WATERFALL AND QUALITY MANAGEMENT

One more problem with the waterfall — the last one for this review, although others could undoubtedly be added — is also a major concern for any good manager. It has to do with a fundamental requirement of modern engineering: quality management.

With its rigid division into steps, which corresponds to a division into specialties, the waterfall leads to a corresponding division of labor:

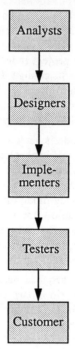

QUALITY CONTROL IN THE TRADITIONAL APPROACH?

This is really the waterfall picture again, reduced to its bare essentials to show the division into teams used, again with some variants, by many companies.

What better recipe could one use to ensure *non*-quality? No one besides the manager has a global view of the product.

The result is easy to predict, and was brilliantly described, more than twenty-five years ago, by a famous computer cartoon reproduced on the adjacent page.

Unfortunately I do not know the exact origin of this picture; if you do, please send it to me, but *only* if your source is older than 1970, since my colleague Jacques André from IRISA has a copy dating back to that time. All I know is that it is as relevant today as it was at the time of its first publication, even if the names of the steps may have to be adapted somewhat.

Such a situation is the natural consequence of the division of labor shown in the above figure. If or rather when something goes wrong, the analyst can put on dignified airs and say: "All my bubbles and arrows were perfect; every bubble had at least one *in* arrow and one *out* arrow; every arrow came from a bubble and went to a bubble. If there is a bug, ask the implementation team. To tell you the truth, I am not surprised. They always mess up my work. What do you expect? These coders don't know how to think."

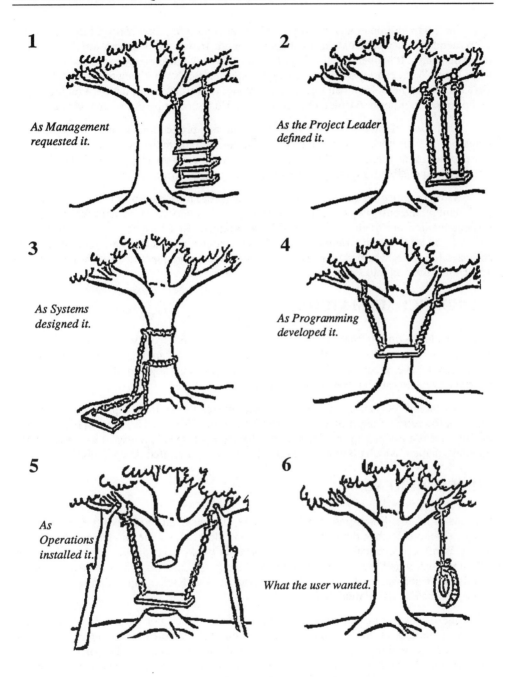

IMPEDANCE MISMATCHES

(Pre-1970 cartoon; origin unknown)

But go to an implementer and you will hear something like: "Sorry, I did my best. I do remember that specification document, though. It was riddled with ambiguities and inconsistencies. It happens all the time: they just give me those messy specs and expect me to fix them. What can I do? After all, I'm just a coder, that's what they tell me all the time. Go ask the designers. Now can I get back to work? A customer says there's a memory leak in the socket routine for 64-bit architectures, and I'd better figure out what's wrong."

This kind of piecemeal approach to industrial production is what brought other industries to their knees, most famously the US automobile industry before it finally came to its senses in the mid-90s. It favors a finger-pointing, buck-passing atmosphere where no one feels responsible for quality. Not surprisingly, quality will not be there.

As other industries (at least those which survived) have painfully learned, often from the Japanese, the only way to obtain quality is to make every team member feel personally responsible for the quality of the resulting product. This idea is the transposition to software of **total quality management**. It will require a radically new approach to the software lifecycle, where the primary decomposition technique will be orthogonal to the waterfall's division into steps.

IMPEDANCE MISMATCHES

The obstacles to quality that have just been analyzed derive from what may be called the "impedance mismatches" of the waterfall model. As in an electrical circuit whose components have incompatible impedances, the various steps in the waterfall cause interface problems at each step through the process.

We should look instead for a scheme that makes the various steps as compatible as possible, focusing on the similarities rather than on the differences. This will lead us, later in this discussion, to explore further the principle of seamlessness, previewed in the previous chapter, which plays a central role in the object-oriented process model.

THE ESCHERFALL

Because of all the difficulties mentioned above, the waterfall model is little more than a pleasant fiction. Rather than the one-directional flow which the model prescribes, the reality is often a cyclical process that irresistibly evokes the picture appearing on the adjacent page, which was drawn with remarkable prescience (as if he had penetrated the moods of the software industry) by the Dutch artist M.C. Escher and which we may in his honor call the Escherfall model.

The Escherfall in fact evokes lifecycle variants found not only in some less-than-optimal practices of the software industry but also in software engineering theory. Introduced by Boehm as a potential replacement for the waterfall, the **spiral model** of software development is a form of iterated waterfall, presented graphically as a spiral of which each revolution represents an analysis-specification-design-implementation sequence — hence the name. Although this idea corrects some of the deficiencies of the waterfall, one cannot in good faith recommend it for object technology, if the focus is on improving productivity and obtaining quality products.

The Escherfall

M.C Escher: *Waterval* (Waterfall),
October 1961.

When we look at prototyping we will have to contend again with the strange idea that
if you are not sure about a strategy for solving a problem then the solution is to apply it two
or more times. But that is for later.

TOWARDS A BETTER MODEL

Enough for now about the deficiencies of the traditional approach, either in its imagined form, the waterfall, or its more realistic variants such as the Escherfall. Is there a better way?

We need a model that does away with the rigidity of the traditional approach, but retains an orderly approach to software construction. The answer is known as the *cluster model* of the software lifecycle and is based on several ideas:

- Seamlessness.

- Reversibility.

- The notion of cluster, which gives the model its name.

- A better integration of design and implementation.

- A new activity: generalization.

SEAMLESSNESS

The waterfall approach emphasizes the differences that exist between successive steps in the lifecycle. This leads to the impedance mismatches pointed out above and, as noted, is a major impediment to the quality of the resulting product.

In contrast, the object-oriented approach emphasizes the fundamental unity of the software development process. From analysis to design, implementation and maintenance, the same issues arise, the same techniques apply, the same mental patterns recur. The method downplays the inevitable differences by providing a unifying framework and a single notation that will accompany the software developer from the beginning to the end of the software process.

This central property of the object-oriented method will be reflected in the graphical representation of the lifecycle model. It will still be useful to distinguish between various project activities; assume that these are analysis, design, implementation and maintenance (although the actual division into phases, defined below, will be somewhat different). A traditional view would use a representation of the form

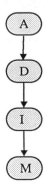

Instead the object-oriented view illustrates the succession of phases through a graphical convention, used below in the diagrams representing the cluster model, which emphasizes the continuity of the process:

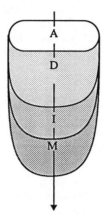

This illustration shows the successive steps not as new endeavors that break with the past (the previous steps), but as successive increments, successive variations on the same theme. Its shape is that of a stalactite, and like a stalactite it builds up (or rather down, but who are we to quibble?) by repeated accretions.

This property is essential to understand the nature of properly applied object-oriented software development. Instead of a succession of separate products, the O-O developer works on a single product, starting from a high-level, abstract view of that product, and then refining it until all its aspects have been properly handled, including the most mundane details of implementation, efficiency and machine adaptation.

> A note is in order here to warn the reader that some of the object-oriented literature, in particular a number of books on object-oriented analysis, take a more timid view and may still leave the impression that analysis, design and implementation are separate tasks. Such presentations often describe "hybrid" approaches in which some object-oriented ideas are introduced on top of earlier approaches such as entity-relationship modeling. Laudable as it may be to introduce new concepts in an evolutionary fashion, it is hard to accept that approaches which renounce seamlessness deserve the O-O label.

REVERSIBILITY

A companion property of seamlessness is reversibility: the idea that the software construction cycle is not always one way, from analysis to design and implementation, but that ideas encountered late in the process can and should influence the earliest stages.

To managers trained in the waterfall culture, this is a subversive idea: it means that programmers can be permitted to change the definition of the system's functionality! But for people who have learned to practice object technology well, there is nothing scary.

Whatever software theories may say, some good ideas will only become clear when you have an implementation. What then are the manager's possible responses?

One can deny this process and forbid the programmers from questioning specifications. This is what happens in organizations that apply rigid waterfall principles, and a strict division of labor such as the one shown on page 44. The result: in addition to the problems discussed above (poor quality resulting from impedance mismatches), the product is likely to suffer from restricted functionality. The manager should not expect, too, to keep competent software developers very long: the best ones will sooner or later migrate *en masse* to a company whose management is more receptive to good ideas. (See also "COSTS AND BENEFITS", page 152.)

One can be more flexible and accept late changes. But if the lifecycle model does not explicitly support this process, you run the risk of ending up with major discrepancies between the results of analysis, design and implementation. How can you guarantee that program changes will be reflected in the analysis and design documents?

In a seamless development process, there is a single product for each component of the software. It contains elements addressing all levels of abstraction, from analysis to implementation. So even for a late change you will be able to update all the affected elements.

This emphasis on reversibility suggests an adaptation of the pictorial representation of step sequencing in the lifecycle, using dotted arrows to show the possible feedback of later phases on results obtained previously:

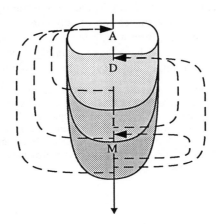

For simplicity and readability, the cluster lifecycle diagrams appearing later in this chapter will not show the dotted backward arrows. But you should consider that they are there, representing the reversible nature of the object-oriented lifecycle, which entitles any step to cause changes that will be reflected in all the earlier steps.

It would be a mistake to confuse this approach with what was labeled the Escherfall above (see page 47) or with the spiral model. Instead of a continuous cycle repeating the same steps, reversibility leads us to consider that we work on a single product, seamlessly enriched as we learn more about our system and add new elements to it.

THE NOTION OF CLUSTER

With the waterfall, you were supposed to perform each activity on the whole system: specification of the full system, design of the full system and so on.

The result is an all or nothing process: either you get everything right, or you get nothing. For a manager preoccupied with risk, this is not acceptable. Too many things can go wrong; too many things *will* go wrong. Individual failures are a normal part of project development. It is unacceptable to let any such failure derail the overall process.

In the cluster model, we divide the system into a number of parts called **clusters**. A cluster may also be called a subsystem or, in some cases, a library. It is a set of classes large enough to provide a major component of the system but small enough to be managed by a small group of people. A typical cluster will have 5 to 40 classes, and will be developed by 1 to 4 people.

> To give another view of size limitations, a cluster must be simple enough to enable a single person, if need be (for example at maintenance time), to understand all of it after at most a few weeks of work. In a large software system, it is impossible for a single person to comprehend everything; at best a person can be familiar with the basic decisions taken throughout the system. The cluster level marks the threshold up to which it must still be possible for one person to master all the details.

Here is an example drawn from a task in which ISE was involved: the design of a Frequent Flyer system for a major airline. Some of the clusters, and some representative classes for each cluster, looked like this:

Example cluster	Representative classes
MEMBERSHIP	*MEMBER* *BENEFICIARY* *STATUS*
OPPORTUNITIES	*BONUS* *REDEMPTION* *AWARD*
TRAVEL	*ROUTE* *SEGMENT* *SERVICE* *BUSINESS_CLASS* *FIRST_CLASS*
SPACE_TIME	*CONTINENT* *TIME_ZONE* *PERIOD*

In the cluster model, we will try to keep a sequential scheme but not for the system as a whole, as that would be far too monolithic. Instead, once the division into clusters has been done, we apply a mini-lifecycle to *each* cluster. The resulting process is a form of **concurrent engineering** illustrated by the figure on the adjacent page.

CONCURRENT ENGINEERING

To read the cluster lifecycle illustration, you need to realize that both the left-to-right and top-to-bottom directions represent increasing time. No, you do not need to learn a new theory of physics; we will return to a linear time scale shortly. The figure's two time axes simply mean that the model specifies a *partial ordering* of activities rather than a single possible order. The partial ordering is the following rule: if step A appears above B and to its left (or at the same horizontal position), then A must be executed before B. If they are at the same vertical position and A is to the left of B, A must be executed first or they may happen concurrently. This leaves the project manager much flexibility as to the precise order in which things will happen, and explicitly allows various activities to occur at the same time.

I have found that some people have difficulty understanding this lack of a single ordering in the picture. Usually they are managers who are so accustomed to linear models of their work as to be reluctant to accept a scheme where they have to find their own itinerary, step by step, for each project. If you are in this category please accept that what you will lose in the simplicity of the theory you will regain in its adaptation to the reality of software project management. The world is not linear; neither is software development.

Here then is how to read the picture. The process begins with a feasibility study; here there is nothing original, since any project must start by asking whether there is really a need for a new software development. The answer may well be no: perhaps a previous project has yielded a system that is good enough for the current need; perhaps you can just buy a product off-the-shelf; perhaps you do not need a software system, but simply a better organization of your company or certain manual procedures.

Assuming some software development is needed (even if it largely relies on reuse and adaptation of existing software), the next step is to divide the project into clusters. More below on how and by whom this should be done.

These first two steps, feasibility study and division into clusters, are the only synchronous, waterfall-like components of the cluster model. After that we switch to a concurrent engineering mode. There are only two ordering constraints, corresponding to the horizontal and vertical dimensions on the picture:

• Each cluster defines a mini-lifecycle, whose activities occur in the order shown by the figure: cluster and class specification, design-implementation, V&V, generalization.

• Clusters are started in the order given: for any i, the first step (specification) of cluster $i + 1$ cannot start earlier than the first step of cluster i.

Within these global constraints you will, as the project leader, find your own scheduling, which depends on your staff resources, on the difficulty of the various tasks involved, and on your customers' requirements. Project management becomes a navigation through the cluster diagram; a sequence of scheduling decisions that will bring the two-dimensional time chart of the cluster model illustration back to the normal form of sequencing — which is of course one-dimensional. So on the subsequent figures the time scale will be linear (from top to bottom), but will allow for parallel activities along the horizontal dimension.

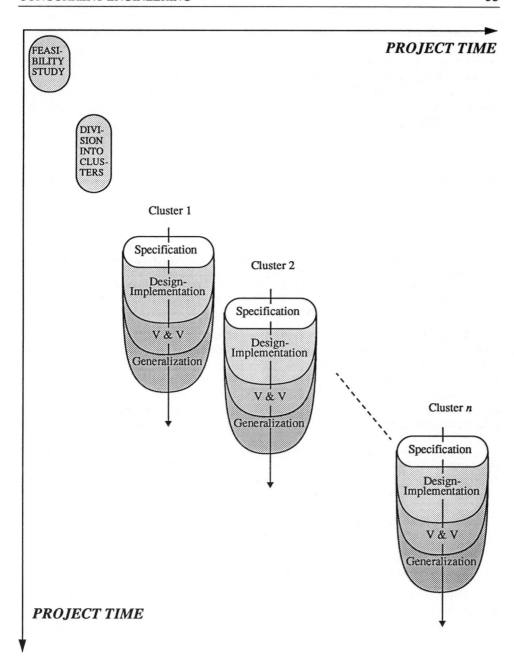

**THE CLUSTER MODEL
OF THE SOFTWARE LIFECYCLE**

One of the consequences of this concurrent engineering approach is the possibility of cluster divergence. Although information hiding, Design by Contract and other object-oriented principles help limit the risk, you should be careful to avoid letting clusters become incompatible with each other even though they individually appear satisfactory. The solution is simple: frequently perform an integration that will bring everything together. The Integration Principle discussed in a later chapter ("THE MANAGER AS INTEGRATOR", page 140) provides a precise guideline.

THE STEPS

The cluster model includes the following steps for the mini-lifecycles associated with each individual cluster.

The **specification** step identifies the classes and defines their official interfaces.

> There is no fundamental difference between the words *specification* and *analysis*, only a cultural difference reflecting the Continental Divide that runs through the software community, both industrial and academic: people who think of themselves as "computing scientists" tend to speak of specification where people who would describe their field as "information systems" or "MIS" would refer to analysis. The rest of this discussion uses the term specification because it is more precise, but analysis would be adequate too.

Design-implementation fills in the class specifications by adding the operational aspects. In contrast with the traditional model, there is no need in object-oriented development to separate design from implementation. All that differs is the level of abstraction: design addresses the general structure of the solution, implementation finishes the details. With a good object-oriented language and a competent development team, there is never a time when you can say "design is over now, we go to implementation"; you proceed imperceptibly from the abstract to the concrete, and back when needed.

Both design and implementation are forms of *programming* in the noblest sense of the term. All that changes is the abstractness of the machine that you program. Implementation means programming the available computer; design means programming a more abstract machine (except in Eiffel, where it is the same machine).

> The "available computer" that we program at the implementation stage is in fact already abstract: programming the physical computer would mean writing a machine program, and who writes machine code or even assembly language these days? The abstract machine that you program is defined by the combination of hardware, operating system, compiler for the chosen programming language and development tools.

Validation & Verification plays the same role as in older approaches. The concern for quality and the practice of quality assurance must apply throughout the project; but there remains the need for a step officially devoted to assessing the result against the objectives.

Generalization is a new step, with no equivalent in traditional methods. It is applicable to companies that are serious about applying the reusability goal to their own developments. The purpose of the generalization step is to extract from the project those *program elements* that hold the best promise of reusability, and transform them into *reusable components*, according to the following definition:

> **DEFINITION: PROGRAM ELEMENT, SOFTWARE COMPONENT**
>
> A program element is a module that is a part of some software system.
>
> A reusable component is a module that has a value of its own, independently from the system for which it may have been originally defined, so that it may be included in a library and used in many different applications.

The presence of the generalization step raises several questions: Why a separate step if we apply reusability concerns throughout the process? Would it be preferable to have a separate team (the library group) take care of generalization, rather than letting each project generalize its own project-specific developments? What technical activities does generalization involve in object-oriented development?

These questions are so essential to the full implementation of object-oriented techniques as to deserve a chapter of their own — chapter 6, which discusses how to make reusability succeed.

> In particular, if your reaction to the concept of generalization has been to note that one should think about reusability from the start, not devote a specific part of the process to it, be sure to read "THE ROLE OF GENERALIZATION", page 125, which shows that both of these approaches are necessary but none is sufficient. On the precise activities required by generalization, see "GENERALIZATION TASKS", page 122.

What counts for the moment is that a company that is serious about object technology and reusability should consider generalization as important a component of its project lifecycle as specification, design-implementation and V&V.

PROJECT MANAGEMENT AND STEP ORDERING

Central to the cluster model is the existence of many different ways to perform the linearization of the two-dimensional scheme — of many different paths through the maze that will take you from start to successful finish.

To show various possibilities, the remaining figures of this chapter have a one-dimensional time axis rather than the two-dimensional structure of the initial cluster illustration of page 53. They correspond to possible linearizations of the general cluster scheme. The appearance of two activities at the same vertical level on one these figures indicates that these activities are meant to be executed concurrently.

Two extreme cases, shown by the figure appearing on the next page, are worth noting:

- At one end, you can decide for a purely synchronous approach: specification of all clusters, then design-implementation of all clusters, and so on. The resulting model is close to the waterfall, with a few differences such as the fusion of design and implementation steps and the introduction of a generalization step. Such a scheme, for which we may perhaps coin the term **clusterfall model**, may be found in organizations having large development groups and a strong waterfall-oriented tradition.

- The opposite variant focuses on one cluster at a time: do cluster 1 from beginning to end, then cluster 2 and so on. This scheme, which may be reasonable for example with a very small team (one person or just a few), may be called the **trickle model** — a trickle being what remains of the waterfall at times of drought.

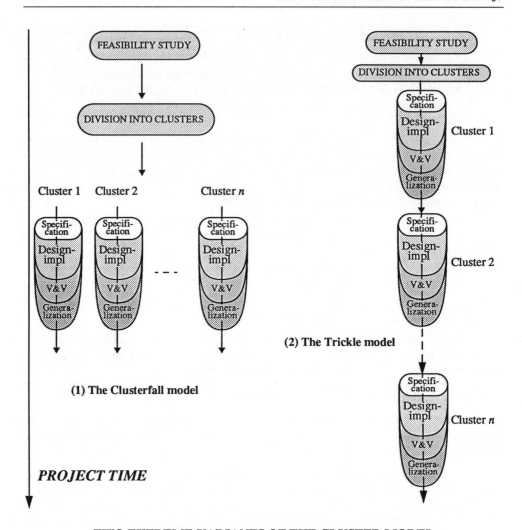

TWO EXTREME VARIANTS OF THE CLUSTER MODEL

Most of the time, however, the task scheduling policy will lie somewhere between the clusterfall and the trickle. You start a few clusters, and then whenever a minicycle step is completed you may decide to proceed to the next step, to resume another cluster that had temporarily been stopped, or to start one of the remaining fresh clusters. Each decision is a function of your resources, of the speed at which you are able to proceed, of the difficulties encountered, and of your assessment of the various risks involved.

The figure on the adjacent page shows an example of such a scheduling, with its mix of sequential and concurrent activities. Unlike the earlier figures this one assumes that the various clusters may proceed at different speeds — as they usually will in practice.

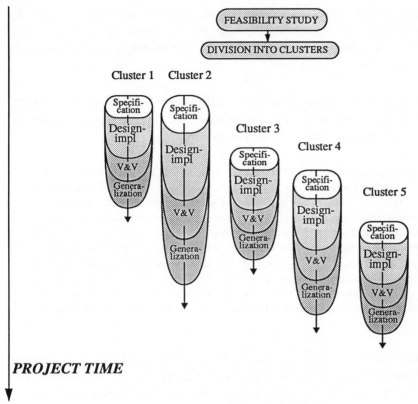

PROJECT TIME

EXAMPLE CLUSTER SEQUENCING

RISK MANAGEMENT AND DYNAMIC RECONFIGURATION

For project managers one of the major advantages of the cluster model is its flexibility, which gives them the indispensable tools of risk management.

With the waterfall the project is at the mercy of any unforeseen circumstance. If the analysis of any single part is delayed by one day, the whole process may be delayed by one day, and the people in charge of subsequent phases — the designers, the implementers, the QA team — will be idle for one more day. If it were possible to predict effort with reasonable accuracy this might be acceptable. But no such prediction is possible in software development.

With all the talk about "software *engineering*" it is easy to forget that any ambitious software development project involves a component, smaller or larger, of *research*. The engineering component is definitely there, making a software project similar in some respects to the construction of a bridge or of an integrated circuit. But in every serious project that I have seen this engineering component was significantly less than 100%. Any such project has to solve problems that have not been solved before. When you build a bridge, you more or less know what to expect: with similar terrain and requirements, bridge B will take about the same effort as bridge A; using your training and experience, and some allowance for various possible delaying factors, you can roughly predict the necessary effort. Not so with software.

The development of a cluster often incurs delays due to problems that had not been foreseen, or are more difficult than had been expected. The reverse also happens: a particular development may proceed faster than planned.

> This unpredictability sets the limit of analogies with bridge building and other engineering professions, bringing instead the image of the mathematician, the theoretical physicist, or other researchers. It is one of the defining properties of software construction, maddening at times — but also part of what makes this discipline so attractive to those who practice it. After all, the term *hacker* (in its original sense of a programmer fanatically devoted to the trade) was coined à propos software development, not road construction or circuit design. No offense is meant here to these engineering specialties and their sisters; many mechanical, chemical and electrical engineers are undoubtedly passionate about their jobs. But the grip that programming holds on so many of its practitioners' minds seems unique, and it is probably due in part to the unpredictability of software development and the frequent appearance of seemingly new problems.

Modern software techniques, in particular the systematic approach to reuse promoted by object technology and by this book, can reduce the unpredictability but not eliminate it — at least not in the near future. For the manager this causes one of the major sources of **risk** in software projects: the risk that a task will proceed significantly slower or faster than planned and destroy the elegant PERT or Gantt charts that were so carefully devised at the beginning of the project.

Here the cluster model provides considerable help. By allowing more than one itinerary through the set of obligatory steps pictured on the figure of page 53, the model allows **dynamic reconfiguration** of the software management process. If a task relative to a certain cluster proves harder than expected, you can decide on the spot to divert resources that had been earmarked for other clusters, either by delaying the start of a new cluster, or by postponing a certain step for a cluster whose initial steps have already been started. Conversely, if a task is completed faster than expected, you can start a new cluster earlier, or proceed faster with a cluster already in progress.

Without this kind of flexibility, the project leader is as helpless as a judge who must work under mandatory sentencing guidelines. The cluster model enables you to do your real job as a manager, taking your responsibilities and making your own reasoned decisions. Of course, not everyone likes having to make tough decisions, which may help explain why people have for so long clung to the Waterfall.

BIBLIOGRAPHY

Barry W. Boehm: *Software Engineering Economics*, Prentice Hall, 1981.

A classic — the first book to examine the economic aspects of software construction; the best presentation of the traditional model of software engineering. Frustrating at times for a reader of the nineteen-nineties because of its restricted view: Boehm's approach to software is what may be called the TRW model — on day one you get 500 million dollars from the Air Force and a requirements document, and the aim of the game is to deliver something two years later without squandering too much of the money. Well, I am exaggerating a bit, but someone who was not familiar beforehand with the software industry would not know from the book that there is such a thing as a mass market of software or a microcomputer industry (both of which, of course, were many times smaller in 1981 than they are today). Do not look for the notion of "product" or for a discussion of reuse. The presentation is all about one-of-a-kind developments, usually huge, and usually for very rich customers. If you are wondering whether to price your latest visual e-mail tool at $14.95, $19.95 or $24.95 (how much for Shipping & Handling?), this is not the place to look at for guidance; but if you are thinking of building your own Coordinated Western Hemisphere Ballistic Missile Control System you might find a tip or two (three billions? or shall we go for four?).

Despite these quibbles I still find *Software Engineering Economics* to be a must read for any software manager. It is filled with figures and reports from actual projects. Its COCOMO model, although based on some controversial premises (lines of code as an a priori estimate of a system's size), is one of the most serious efforts so far to classify the sources of cost in software development. I am eagerly waiting for a second edition that will integrate the changes in software technology since the nineteen-sixties.

Kim Waldén and Jean-Marc Nerson: *Seamless Object-Oriented Software Architecture...**

(See full reference on page 38.) Among the books on object-oriented analysis, this is the one that (with Henderson-Sellers and Edwards, also cited on page 38) most emphasizes seamlessness; it also explores the notion of reversibility in depth.

On the cluster model:

The model was discussed at some length in my article *The New Culture of Software Development: Reflections on the Practice of Object-Oriented Design*, in TOOLS 89 (Technology of Object-Oriented Languages and Systems), Angkor/SOL, Paris, November 1989, pages 13-23.

The original ideas came from an article of Cyrille Gindre and Frédérique Sada, first available in French in 1987, which described and discussed an early successful object-oriented project at Thomson-CSF. An English version was published as *A Development in Eiffel: Design and Implementation of a Network Simulator* in the *Journal of Object-Oriented Programming*, vol. 2, no. 2, May 1989, pages 27-33. Both this article and *The New Culture...* also appear, slightly revised, in the book *Advances in Object-Oriented Software Engineering**, eds. Dino Mandrioli and B. Meyer, Prentice Hall, 1992.

4

But what about prototyping?

It is commonly believed that object-oriented development favors or even implies prototyping; this is indeed one of the buzzwords commonly associated with the method. But if you do not remember encountering it in the previous chapter, it is not that you have missed anything. It is simply that it was not there, and for a good reason: prototyping has nothing to do with object technology.

We must of course explore this point a bit deeper. As it often turns out, analyzing a bad idea and trying to understand why it is bad provides insights into what we should really be doing. And we will discover an unexpected application of the idea of prototyping to software engineering — the only one that really makes sense, but also the only one that none of the available literature seems to have hit upon so far.

A BORROWED TERM

The first task is to find out what the term "prototyping" really means. One of the major problems in assessing this notion is indeed that it is often poorly defined if at all. And it is likely that if the first paragraph above made you scream that the author was crazy and throw the book on the floor then you have a different definition of what a prototype means. (The rest of this chapter assumes that you picked up the book in a still usable condition.)

Is it appropriate to talk about prototypes in software? After all, this is not a new term but one with a long history in other industries — mechanical, electrical, electronic. In those areas a prototype is a fully functional product, which only differs from the final product through either (sometimes both) of two properties:

- The prototype has been custom-built, whereas the final product is intended to be mass-produced. This may be called a **mass-production** prototype.

- The prototype works on a smaller scale than the final product. This may be called a **reduced-scale** prototype.

An example of mass production prototype is a prototype for a new car. An example of reduced-scale prototype is a water-processing plant using a new process, but capable of processing a few cubic meters a day rather than the thousands of cubic meters necessary to handle the water needs of a big city.

In both cases the designers expect that the prototype, although intended to provide all the needed functions, may still contain a few defects, whereas the discovery of defects in the final product would be a much graver event. The purpose of prototyping is precisely to extirpate defects at much less effort than for a product which is already produced in large numbers with the consequent investment in machinery and processes (mass-production prototype), or has been built to full scale at great expense (reduced-scale prototype).

In both cases, too, no one expects the prototype to be kept: once it has fulfilled its purpose by allowing the testing of a number of hypotheses, it will simply be discarded. A car manufacturer will not recycle the prototype of a new car into the mass production process; and it is hard to imagine that a water processing company, having built a prototype plant capable of handling the water needs of a village, would move the plant to Tokyo and expand its facilities so as to process the water for eight million people.

How does this traditional notion of prototype transpose to software construction? Simple question, simple answer: there is no direct equivalent. This applies to both cases:

- Mass-production prototypes would be meaningless in software since the duplication process (diskettes, CDs, manuals) is the easiest and cheapest part of the problem — and usually is not even considered part of the *software* engineering process.

- As for reduced-scale prototypes, it is indeed wise to try a software system on a small scale (for example testing a communication system on three local computers before you use it on a wide-area network), but this is not prototyping: if the techniques used (software architecture, algorithms, data structures, use of hardware resources) scale up, possibly after some tuning, the initial software and the final version are essentially the same. If the techniques do not scale up, the whole initial effort may have been wasted. All it will have taught you, for a rather expensive price, is that the approach used is not adequate. This is a failed experiment, not a prototype.

In view of all this, it is surprising that anyone should ever use the word "prototyping" for software development. So we have to look further.

PROTOTYPING IN SOFTWARE

Software people do talk about prototyping, of course. What do they actually mean?

Closer examination reveals that in software the term is used, or misused, with four possible meanings:

1 • In some cases, it simply denotes an experiment. You want to know if a certain user interface idea will please your users; if a certain algorithm will be faster than another; if you can tune the organization of a large data structure to reduce paging. You just try the idea and examine the result. This technique may simply be called **experimentation**.

2 • In a somewhat related use of the term, pilot projects serving to try out a new method (such as the object-oriented method) or new tools are sometimes called prototypes. Such projects, although often small, are for real, and are intended to yield useful products. The major difference with a non-pilot project is that some of the usual constraints may be removed; for example the hardware may be different from what is usually imposed. There is also the implicit recognition that the pilot project is more likely to fail than a normal development. But such projects are not prototypes in any ordinary sense of the term; one does intend to keep the results. This discussion will refer to them under the name **pilot projects**. (A section of this book is devoted to the issue of how to choose and plan pilot projects in the transition to object technology; see "PILOT PROJECTS", page 82.)

3 • Some people also use the term "prototyping" in a quite different sense: to denote a development process where you build a certain self-contained part of the system first, and add subsequent elements later. For example you may want to start by implementing the major functionalities but with a very crude user interface, or even no user interface at all (the functionalities being accessible only from other software elements); then you add new functionalities, including one or more user interfaces. This technique is sometimes called "incremental prototyping", but it really has nothing to do with prototyping in any meaningful sense of the term; we may call it **incremental development**.

4 • What is probably the most common use of the word "prototyping" covers something quite different again: the suggestion that before building the final version of a system you should build a provisional one, learn from the results, and then restart from ground zero. This is often known as *throwaway prototyping*; the phrase "rapid prototyping" is often used. (In my experience, "slow prototyping" is often a more accurate a posteriori description of the method, but people do not know that beforehand.) This last case corresponds, in standard engineering disciplines, to **mockups**. Unlike a prototype, a mockup is not a temporary version of the final product; it often does not employ the same materials, and is not adequate for normal use. It merely serves to test a number of hypotheses regarding the product and its construction process. This is exactly what throwaway prototypes are about.

The first three techniques clearly have a place in the software development process. Experiments can be necessary to answer questions that are not amenable to analytical treatment. Pilot projects are a sensible way to try out a new approach and study how to adapt it to the context of a specific company. Incremental development makes it possible to proceed in stages and obtain partial solutions along the way — less and less partial as the development progresses. This idea is essential to reducing risk and played a central role in the cluster model as discussed in the previous chapter.

All these ideas are fine, and if your view of prototyping corresponds to any one of them, there is nothing wrong with it, although one may quibble with the terminology. It is dangerous to use a well-established term in a meaning that is radically different from the accepted one. The simple and precise terms *experiment*, *pilot project* and *incremental development* are the appropriate ones to characterize the three techniques discussed. Calling them "prototyping" only creates confusion.

THE POTEMKIN APPROACH TO SOFTWARE DEVELOPMENT

The real trouble is with the fourth and most common use of the word prototyping: mockups (for which the rest of this chapter will continue to use the term "throwaway prototype" because it is more common in the literature). Prototyping in this sense is one of those ideas which have come to be considered so obviously good that people tend to skip any rational analysis of whether it actually contributes anything.

The most often quoted line about throwaway prototypes comes from Fred Brooks's popular collection of essays, *The Mythical Man-Month*. (Brooks was the chief architect of OS/360, and the book draws on the lesson of that experience.) Brooks offers the advice

Plan to throw one away; you will, anyhow.

This argument contains its own negation: what is so magical about the number one? If we expect the first attempt to fail, how do we know that the second will succeed? Should we plan to throw two away, or three, or four?

But the flaw in this approach is more fundamental. Throwaway prototyping assumes that by dropping a number of requirements we can develop software that will teach us something useful. This ignores the whole reason why software development is difficult: the need to reconcile a whole set of quality requirements.

Good software must be correct, robust, efficient, reusable, extendible, portable, easy to use, easy to learn, self-protecting, rich in functions. Individually, these requirements may be tough; but collectively they are even tougher. Often, they conflict with each other: efficiency, which suggests specialization, fights portability and reusability, which suggest generalization; ease of use fights self-protection; richness of functions fights ease of learning. Much of the hard work in building a software system involves reconciling these goals or, when they cannot be fully reconciled, finding acceptable tradeoffs.

If you focus on one or just a few of the requirements, the task becomes much easier. This is typically what we do for a throwaway prototype: we sacrifice efficiency, or ease of use, or extendibility, or portability, or some of the richer functionality, so as to get something out quickly. But when we get that result and it is successful we may just be fooling ourselves, and our financial backers too: how do we know that the effort has helped us in any way towards the final product? Perhaps we were able to produce an easy-to-use system *only* because we removed the efficiency requirement, or an efficient system *only* because we removed the portability requirement.

If that is the case we will just have wasted our time and their money. When we start the real product we will have gained nothing; we may in fact have made the real development longer by encouraging it to use solutions that were appropriate for the throwaway prototype, but will not work for the real thing because of the constraints that we had ignored.

The most effective step I know towards a solution is the one so strongly emphasized in this book, together with other object-oriented techniques: reuse. To handle difficult software projects, one should rely, as much as possible, on existing software components, which previous efforts have developed, validated and repeatedly improved.

Throwaway prototyping evokes the memory of Prince Grigori Aleksandrovitch Potemkin, Field Marshall and secret jusband of Catherine the Great of Russia, who in order to please his Empress during the Crimea expedition of 1787 would have workers repaint the façades, and only the façades, in the villages she was due to visit. People try prototyping precisely because the development of an ambitious system seems so difficult. But this is a mirage. Prototyping will only delay the day of reckoning; it is part of the problem, not of the solution.

THROWAWAY PROTOTYPING VERSUS QUALITY

The worst aspect of throwaway prototypes is that they discourage professionalism and quality.

Software quality is largely (although not only) in the details. To produce good software, you must think about myriad cases — everything that could go wrong, every novice who will press a meaningless sequence of keys, every user who will not have read the manual (or will not even know that there *is* a manual), every other software product that will be used in connection with yours, every strange hardware configuration, every potential bug in the supporting platform. This task of getting everything right to the last dot on the last *i* is hard, unglamorous, sometimes tedious. Every step of the effort achieves only a little improvement of the eventual product; but together these steps will make a world of difference — the difference between so-so software and a quality product.

Developers will only make this effort if they feel it is worthwhile; for a throwaway prototype, they usually will not. Why bother if the whole thing is going to be discarded anyway? Why spend your evenings and weekends thinking about elegant solutions? Why worry about hundreds of little features, often tricky or boring, that might turn a decent sketch into a successful product? Let the next team take care of that!

I once observed an enthusiastic team being told by a freshly hired manager that, by the way, what they were building would only be used as a throwaway prototype, and a new development would take over. The reaction was predictable: morale, productivity and quality plummeted at once. No one was interested any more.

A cynic would derive the following advice from these observations: even if you are using throwaway prototyping, never tell the developers.

Even if the manager succeeds in keeping the development team interested, throwaway prototyping raises a major risk management issue. The task of the manager, as noted in the previous chapter, is to focus on risk areas and, for this purpose, to make sure that the tough problems get all the attention they deserve early in the project. With throwaway prototyping, the reverse will occur. A team that knows that its job is not "for real" will naturally be tempted to work on the parts that have the highest GSR (Glitz-to-Sweat Ratio), those which produce the most impressive effect for the least possible work. Obscure foundational elements (parts that would form the spine of a real production system, but require long work for little immediately visible effect) will be put aside. The danger exists, then, of producing a beautiful prototype for a system that cannot realistically be built, or can only be built at a considerable cost which the prototyping effort does not reveal.

Prototyping, in this case, almost becomes a form of cheating. The team makes an impressive presentation of the prototype with the unspoken implication that its best features can be transposed to a real system; but there is no proof of this implication:

THE PROTOTYPING RULE

A successful prototype proves only one thing: that you can produce a prototype.

SHIPPING THE PROTOTYPE

Cheating sometimes works. With a flashy prototype, you might actually convince someone! If that someone happens to be in a decision-making position, you might find yourself a victim of the famous curse, *"May you get what you hope for!"*: after a successful demo, you may be expected to deliver what you have shown.

One of our customers, from a large bank, once told me about such a case in one of their company's earlier projects. An impressive throwaway prototype was put together and shown to the CEO. The CEO was duly impressed; everyone was happy. A week later, a major business newspaper carried an interview of the CEO, where the product was announced as imminent — a key tool in the company's competitive strategy. It was too late to educate higher management about the difference between reality and make-believe in software development: orders were already starting to come in! A crash project had to be put together to try to build a product. Needless to say, that project took many months to complete, and a lot of people, managers and developers alike, went through pretty rough times.

Flashy demos are not the only incentive for shipping a throwaway prototype. There may be budget restrictions, which make it unlikely that the full project can be funded at the level originally planned, and lead the purse string holders to suggest that perhaps we should just deliver what we already have; there may be the urge to ship *something* in response to market demand or competition; there may be the feeling that enough money has already been spent — rapid prototyping is always prototyping, but is not always rapid.

If the pressures succeed and you do ship the prototype, the result is usually disastrous. A product that was never meant to be delivered ends up on the customers' desks. For all the reasons discussed above, the quality will generally be unacceptable.

DISTINGUISHING THE VARIANTS

Considering the possibility that we might be asked to ship the prototype, and the consequences of such an event, provides a good opportunity to help distinguish between the various kinds of development scheme to which the term "prototyping" is commonly applied. The preceding sections have focused on mockups, or throwaway prototypes. Earlier in this chapter we encountered three legitimate techniques that are often mistakenly characterized as prototyping: experiments, pilot projects and incremental development. It is illuminating to transpose the above question, "Is there a risk that we could be tempted to ship the prototype?", to each of these techniques:

- For an *experiment*, the question would not arise: an experiment only addresses a specific property of the eventual system; the goal may be to help elicit some of the requirements from the users, to assess what kind of user interface they would like, or to try some implementation techniques. But no one would think of shipping the experiment, as it would be useless by itself. This observation actually provides a practical test to distinguish whether a certain suggested scheme is an experiment (legitimate) or a throwaway prototype (useless or harmful).

- For a *pilot project*, not only is it acceptable to ship the result, but that is what you expect to do; if you cannot, it means the pilot project has failed. A pilot project is not meant to be thrown away; it is, as noted, similar to a normal project in most respects, although it has a secondary goal (testing some technological solution) along with its primary one (building a system), and may have a somewhat higher expectation of failure than usual.

- In *incremental development*, you may in some cases discuss the possibility of shipping the project's partial results at some intermediate point — what in a later chapter will be called the "current demo" (see "THE MANAGER AS DEMO KEEPER", page 141). But unlike a throwaway prototype, a partial version is not make-believe; it is the real thing, only incomplete. Whether you can ship it as an advance version to an impatient customer or hot prospect simply becomes a question of how much of the final functionality you believe you have implemented, and how close, in your opinion, the implemented part is to its final form — if it is too immature, it could cause the reverse of the intended effect.

It is particularly important to avoid the confusion between throwaway prototypes and experiments. A typical example, often used to promote prototyping, arises in the area of user interfaces: this is the case in which you try out several user interface ideas before the system is built; often you will involve future users in the evaluation process, with the added benefit that you get them interested early. But this is a simple user interface experiment, not a prototype! The difference is the same as between a Potemkin village and the stage set for *The Bartered Bride* (which also represents a village): in the second case, no one is pretending that there is anything behind the façades.

> Such user interface experiments are bound to become more and more mundane affairs anyway. Modern object-oriented tools make it possible to devise powerful user interfaces with relatively little effort; they can be applied either when the system's main functionality has already been implemented, or ahead of that functionality.

Similarly, the use of small operational models to help users define what they want is not prototyping. This is a "what if...?" form of requirements analysis: when discussing the planned system with future users, you do not just give them abstract descriptions but show them actual scenarios, possibly with the help of computer simulation tools that display a more realistic view of what you have in mind. Although not a substitute for rational analysis and careful design, such techniques are often useful. But in no way can they be called prototyping; they are experiments meant to help design small individual aspects of the envisioned system.

THE SECOND-SYSTEM EFFECT

In debunking throwaway prototyping it is useful to note the contradiction that exists between the *"plan to throw one away"* dictum and another, more perceptive observation appearing elsewhere in Brooks's *Mythical Man-Month* and relating to a phenomenon that he calls the Second System Effect.

The Second System Effect occurs after the success of the first major project undertaken by a developer or a team in a certain area. Often, that first project was carried out under limited resources and tight deadlines; the novelty of the task naturally demanded caution and restraint. As a result, the developers had to limit themselves to the essentials — and come up with a compact, economical, cogent design.

If the project is successful (perhaps *because* of these very limitations, although at the time one usually feels that success was achieved in spite of them), the team may be asked to produce a new, enhanced system; with vastly increased resources, and a matching increase in arrogance, they end up developing a product — the Second System — that is huge and baroque, being loaded with "frills and embellishments" that may actually render it unpleasant or impossible to use. IBM's OS 360, for example, was a Second System for most of its designers.

This analysis is confirmed by the evolution of many systems that start out small and elegant, only to be overtaken by fat (also known in programmers' lore as *creeping featurism*) and, in more than a few cases, succumb to an overdose of cholesterol.

But how then can one suggest to "throw one away"? Surprisingly enough (since the two ideas appear within pages of each other in Brooks's classic book) no one in the software engineering literature seems to have pointed out the contradiction between this precept and the reality of the Second System Effect.

PROTOTYPING AND FAILURE

Does the rejection of throwaway prototyping mean that it is never appropriate to discard a temporary result and restart from scratch?

Of course not. Software developers and managers make mistakes. When you have tried something and it does not work, the best solution may indeed be to admit your failure, throw everything to the wastebasket, and start again on a fresh basis, hoping that the experience has made you wiser. (At ISE we have certainly had our share of such false starts and wasted attempts.)

But there is a difference between starting afresh when you recognize failure, and *planning* to fail the first time! The first decision simply demonstrates the courage to own up to your mistakes; the second, relying on the vague hope that failing once will make the second attempt succeed, is no more than a sloppy development practice and encouragement to postpone thinking about the difficult problems.

The manager should always be ready to recognize a dead end, but should never start a project with the intention of discarding its result.

> **THE PROTOTYPING PRINCIPLE**
>
> Prototyping is always an admission of failure.

THE BELATED VOICE OF REASON

"Plan to throw one away" is often quoted in the software literature; it is hard for example to open an issue of *IEEE Software* that does not extol the virtues of prototyping. In the object-oriented community too, regrettably, many trainers and speakers go around citing Brooks's original advice with all due reverence.

What no one seems to have noticed is that the original author of that advice now knows better.

I was amused to read in a Usenet on-line forum a report about a lecture given in November 1991 at the Swiss Federal Polytechnic Institute in Zürich (ETH) by Fred P. Brooks. The theme of the lecture was *"The Mythical Man-Month Revisited"* and it offered Professor Brooks an opportunity to reflect on the ideas first published in his book sixteen years before. The talk's parts were: *Introduction*; *Where I was wrong*; *Where the world has changed*; *Positions I still hold strongly*; *What I have learned new*. According to the summary posted on the *comp.software-eng* newsgroup (an electronic forum on software engineering issues) on 13 February 1993 by René Schaad from ETH Zürich, here is some of what Brooks had to say as part of the *Where I was wrong* section:

> *"Plan to throw one away"* : *I would now recommend this for bad teams only. I now suggest that you make schedules based on your team's previous experience. My new approach: incremental software engineering, in other words build a small functionally limited but working system and then expand it.*

It is hard to imagine a clearer rejection of the reliance on throwaway prototyping for software development.

The comment that throwaway prototyping can still be used by "bad teams" is a little bewildering, as if implying that a bad team will become good the second time around. Note that the above is only a summary of notes taken by one of the attendees to the talk, and that Brooks may have been more specific in his presentation. Perhaps by "bad" he really meant "inexperienced with the technology being used for the project".

While Brooks himself has realized the dangers of throwaway prototyping, many people have not learned yet, and continue to spread this irresponsible encouragement to poor project management.

PROTOTYPING FOR REUSABILITY?

As noted at the beginning of this chapter ("A BORROWED TERM", page 61), the term "prototyping" is used in software with meanings that bear little connection to its conventional use in engineering. In object technology, however, one activity comes remarkably close to traditional prototyping — although it is not commonly identified as prototyping.

One of the traditional forms of prototype analyzed earlier was the mass-production prototype, defined as "custom-built, whereas the final product is intended to be mass-produced". This was dismissed as having no equivalent in software, where the mass-production process is trivial and is not really a software engineering task.

But wait a minute! If we embrace object technology and adopt its focus on reuse and libraries, then we *do* have a mass-production process, or something that looks remarkably like it. The equivalent of a *custom-built* product is what was called a program element in the discussion of the cluster lifecycle model (see "THE STEPS", page 54): a module that is tailored to the needs of a particular application. The equivalent of a mass-produced artefact is a reusable module meant to be used by many applications: what was called a *software component* and contrasted with program elements.

Before releasing a reusable library to the world, you will want to try its components on a number of specific projects. As will be discussed in more detail in the chapter on reuse (see the A Posteriori Principle, page 117), no class is reusable until it has been reused; the first few attempts at reuse may uncover limitations or deficiencies of the class for its intended role as component of a widely distributed library.

Here prototyping in the mass-production sense has a direct software counterpart. If words taken from ordinary language and applied to software are to have any meaning at all, this is what we can legitimately call prototyping: prototyping a library by trying its components on a few specific developments. This is not so different from the process of trying a few prototypes of a new airplane model on test flights before you start building many instances for delivery to airlines.

The analogy is not perfect: as noted, non-software prototypes are meant to be discarded, whereas if we find some deficiency in a reusable class we will improve the class, not throw it away. But it is a closer analogy than any of the standard uses of prototyping discussed above.

Unfortunately we will have to refrain from using the word "prototyping" in this sense, as it would conflict with by now well-established uses of the term, mostly in the throwaway sense. But the preceding observations should help you understand where the real analogies are between software and other forms of engineering, as opposed to cases where imported terminology is just a source of confusion and mistakes.

PROTOTYPING FOR SOFTWARE: AN ASSESSMENT

It is useful to summarize this discussion of one of today's most popular software ideas. Here are the main points to remember:

- The word "prototyping" as applied to software is misleading (except in the meaning just discussed, which is not generally accepted). It should be avoided altogether.

- Small experiments in various areas, meant to test specific hypotheses, are useful in software development as in any technical development.

- Pilot projects are often useful to evaluate new technology. They should have the same focus on quality as normal projects.

- Incremental software construction is an excellent technique. It is a central part of the cluster model of object-oriented development.

- Mockups (throwaway prototypes) are a waste of time and effort, and directly contradict the goal of software quality.

- The only area of object-oriented software development which evokes a clear analogy with prototyping is the activity of trying out candidate software components in various applications while preparing them for release as part of a reusable library.

One last comment. Why has throwaway prototyping come to be associated with object orientation? The idea of such a close connection can be traced to some of the object-oriented literature of the nineteen-eighties which often advocated throwaway prototyping. The reason was largely circumstantial, resulting from the limitations of early O-O systems (which lacked static typing and could not generate efficient code). The connection has come to be accepted as a fact by many people. But this should not mislead us. All four combinations are possible: O-O with prototyping, non-O-O without prototyping and so on. The view that the two concepts are closely related is the result of specific circumstances in the development of the field. On further analysis the connection just fades away.

The original "plan to throw one away" dictum is dangerous advice, encouraging useless developments, false expectations and waste of resources. That it is so widely revered makes it all the more harmful.

BIBLIOGRAPHY

Fred P. Brooks: *The Mythical Man-Month*, Addison-Wesley, 1974.

A series of short essays on software engineering and project management, based on Brooks's experience as lead designer of IBM's OS 360. Widely considered a classic (how many other computer books from 1974 are still selling?). Two seminal ideas that it introduced are the Second-System Effect (see page 68 in the present chapter) and the so-called Brooks's Law (which will be discussed in "CRISIS REMEDY", page 133).

5

Managing the transition

Starting to develop software with the object-oriented method, although not a complete change of context, is a major technology advance, with many managerial and technical implications. To be successful, you must proceed with your eyes open, and plan. This chapter should help you make all the right moves.

The discussion will cover planning for the move to object technology, training developers and managers, evaluating potential trainers and consultants, choosing pilot projects, and staffing object-oriented projects.

PLANNING

Perhaps the most important aspect of planning for the use of object technology is to know what your goals are. Filling in the questionnaire of the following two pages will help you understand what you are seeking from object technology, and where you now stand.

A few explanations. Question 1 will help you assess your goals. Question 2 addresses your current exposure to object technology; note that use of object-oriented analysis and design with no continuation to implementation and maintenance does not count, but use of object-like approaches such as Ada does. Level 2.5 takes into account the use of hybrid languages, but only if object-oriented techniques were used, since it is possible for example to use a C++ compiler but program in the C subset of the language, which does not qualify as object-oriented experience. If you are at level 2.7 or 2.8, you started the transition already quite some time ago, but some of the lessons of this chapter should still be useful.

If you answer "yes" to 3.2, your choices will be constrained by the choices of your software providers. If you answer "no" to both 3.1 and 3.2, you have both in-house and external developments, and unless you can keep them independent you will need to think about the consistency between your choices and those of your providers.

At the end of this chapter you will find a discussion of how to use the results (see "APPENDIX: INTERPRETING THE QUESTIONNAIRE", page 97). The reason for postponing this interpretation to the chapter's end is to encourage you to fill in the answers first, without knowing the intended interpretation.

THE *OBJECT SUCCESS* QUESTIONNAIRE

1 What are your major goals in considering object technology?

Rate these reasons in order of decreasing value to you, starting with 1 for the most important. If one of them does not apply to your case, do not rate it. Before answering make sure you have read all the reasons listed. Disregard letters in brackets, such as [A].

[A]   1.1 __ Following the general evolution of the software industry.

[D]   1.2 __ Reducing maintenance costs.

[E]   1.3 __ Reducing debugging time.

[F]   1.4 __ Benefiting from external libraries of reusable components.

[B]   1.5 __ Benefiting from an advanced development environment.

[D]   1.6 __ Making the resulting software easier to modify.

[A]   1.7 __ Remaining compatible with the evolution of some of your business partners (such as customers, suppliers, hardware vendors, software houses).

[C]   1.8 __ Quickly producing partial experimental versions ("prototypes") of new products, to assess some of their properties before starting the final versions.

[F]   1.9 __ Capitalizing on your software efforts by making the results more reusable.

[B]   1.10 __ Improving time-to-market for new products.

[E]   1.11 __ Preventing the appearance of bugs.

[B]   1.12 __ Decreasing software development costs.

2 What is your company's current exposure to object technology?

Choose one (the highest number that applies):

    2.0 - Novice level.

    2.1 - Some people have general knowledge about object technology, but no one has had any significant practice.

    2.2 - Some people have used object-like technology, for example by programming in Ada and using associated design techniques, in earlier projects — either within the company or elsewhere.

    2.3 - Some people have used object technology in earlier projects that included implementation in an object-oriented language (not just analysis or design) but the company has not completed any such project.

    2.4 - The company has successfully completed at least one small project (300 classes or less) using object-oriented techniques in an object-oriented language.

    2.5 - The company has successfully completed at least one significant project (more than 300 classes), using object-oriented techniques, in a hybrid object-oriented language such as C++ or CLOS.

    2.6 - The company has successfully completed at least one significant project (as defined above) in a pure object-oriented language such as Eiffel or Smalltalk.

THE *OBJECT SUCCESS* QUESTIONNAIRE
(continued)

2.7 - The company has been developing software using object-oriented techniques in a pure object-oriented language for two or more years, and has successfully completed a number of significant projects with it.

2.8 - Same as 2.7, but for five or more years.

3 What is your company's current software process?

3.1 - Does your company develop most of its software itself?

3.2 - Does your company subcontract most of its software to an outside source (software house, MIS department of the parent company)?

3.3 - Do you have a recommended software process model? (Circle one.)

    3.3.1 No standard process model.

    3.3.2 Waterfall or similar.

    3.3.3 Spiral.

    3.3.4 Prototyping-based.

    3.3.4 Cluster.

    3.3.6 Other _____.

3.4 - What techniques dominate your software process? (Circle one or more.)

    3.4.1 No systematic software technique.

    3.4.2 Structured analysis.

    3.4.3 Merise.

    3.4.4 JSD/JSP.

    3.4.5 Modular ("object-based", as in Ada-oriented approaches).

    3.4.6 Object-oriented.

    3.4.5 Other _____.

3.5 - What is the most common type of qualification among your software developers? (Circle one or, for a more precise answer, give percentages for each category. "Computing science education" includes formal training in programs whose possible official names include such variants as *computer science*, *computer engineering* and *information systems*.)

    3.5.1 No university-level education.

    3.5.2 University-level education but not in computing science.

    3.5.3 B.S. or equivalent (about 4 university years) in computing science.

    3.5.4 Masters' degree or equivalent (5 or 6 years) in computing science.

    3.5.5 PhD in computing science.

    3.5.6 Other _____.

GOING ALL THE WAY

A general advice may be given to any business considering the use of object-oriented techniques:

> ### SERIOUSNESS PRINCIPLE
>
> If you decide to use object orientation, even for trial purposes, apply the method all the way: from analysis to design, implementation and maintenance.

If you are still unsure about the introduction of objects into your company, you might be tempted for your first project to use O-O analysis only. Don't. That would not teach you anything significant. The object-oriented method is meant to be applied seamlessly to an entire project, using an object-oriented language.

Not everyone is ready to undertake an O-O project, even if it is only a pilot project. If you are not ready, wait. But if you do it, do it all the way, and do it well.

INITIAL TRAINING

To succeed you will need to train the people involved in the transition. This includes not just the software developers but also the managers.

Let us first look at developer training. (For the complementary part of the training program see "TRAINING THE MANAGERS", page 79.) The discussion will assume a group of professional software developers, all with some experience, although they may not have used object-oriented techniques before. It will only consider the question of training in an industrial environment; the matter of how and where to integrate object orientation in a university curriculum is also important but belongs elsewhere (see the discussion of the *Object-Oriented Curriculum* article in the bibliography to this chapter, page 103).

Training competent software developers in object technology should be a matter of weeks, not months. Initial training, in particular, should not take more than two weeks. If you are offered a program requiring developers to be trained for any longer initial period before they can start writing O-O software, there is probably something wrong with either the trainers or the variant of object technology that they are promoting.

A typical initial training program will include the following two basic courses:

• Introduction to object technology (at ISE we call this course *Object-Oriented Software Construction* after the name of the textbook that we use): two to three days.

• Hands-on O-O practice: two to four days.

In our experience this is enough to get started. With some object-oriented languages you will need an extra language-specific course, two or three days.

We mostly use Eiffel, for which an elementary language course is not needed; the language follows directly from the method, with a light syntactical baggage. So we teach the notation as part of the above two courses. We offer an "Advanced Eiffel" course for people who have already gained some experience — although here too the emphasis is less on language per se than on advanced object-oriented techniques.

WHAT TO TEACH FIRST

The above list does not include object-oriented analysis. It is a common misconception that one should teach that topic first. It should be included in the curriculum at some stage, and will find a place later in this discussion; but starting with it will lead to disaster. The reasons are not hard to understand:

- The well-understood part of object technology is design and implementation. O-O analysis is an immature field, with many contradictory approaches, none of which has proved itself on a large scale. (As an example the second edition of one of the best known books advocates a method that significantly differs from the one promoted in the first, and its author is now announcing a merge with a formerly competing approach.) In fact, at the time of writing, the second-generation methods, which at last are showing some signs of a systematic, scientific approach, have only started to come out. In contrast, O-O design and implementation, although still a new area, is better understood and backed by successful practical experience.

- For many software developers trained in traditional approaches the key innovation of object technology will be the ideas of seamlessness and reversibility: the realization that you can handle an entire software development, from initial concept to full operation, as a single thread relying on the same techniques and the same notation, and that downstream activities can provide feedback on analysis and design. If you teach them O-O analysis, they will just look at it as a replacement for structured analysis or any other analysis technique they were previously using, then do business as usual for the rest of the development, leaving in the impedance mismatches that characterized earlier approaches. Put more bluntly: they will not get it.

- More generally, it is possible to understand object technology without understanding O-O analysis; but no one can claim to know the technology who does not know how to implement object-oriented software. The proof of the pudding is in the implementation.

THE BOOSTER SHOTS

Regardless of how big your initial training budget is, a rule applies: you should not spend more than 50% of it on the initial courses. The rest should be earmarked for later sessions meant in part to cover more advanced topics but, even more importantly, to go over the initial material again.

In fact the advice that can be given to companies that enquire about training goes further:

> ### THE INITIAL TRAINING SEQUENCE
> Take the initial training courses.
> Then try your hand at object-oriented development.
> Then take the initial training courses.

To some customers, not surprisingly, this will first look like a marketing ploy to make them buy the same thing twice. But that is not the point. The reason for suggesting a duplicate session of the initial courses is that in many cases the first session will only succeed in setting the right mood; only after having practiced the technology, or tried to practice it, will the trainees really understand what the issues are, so that the second session will succeed in getting the concepts through for good.

This problem is particularly acute in today's object-oriented scene, because of what may be called the **mOOsak phenomenon**. It is a rare software person these days who has not been exposed to some kind of description of object orientation. The people you are training will feel familiar with the background object music (the mOOzak), and recognize some of the words as they fly around their ears: *object, class, polymorphism, dynamic binding, multiple inheritance...* As you teach the concepts the first time, the risk exists that the trainees will not grasp the full implications of these concepts and how they can affect their own software. Not that the initial training is unnecessary: it defines the context, and gets people started. But it is not sufficient.

The second time around, the students will have started to grapple with the concrete issues of building O-O software — the ones that arise all the time when you start solving an actual software problem, although they may seem simple or academic when you are listening to a presentation or doing a preset exercise: do I need a class for this concept, or should I just add a feature to an existing class? Is this inheritance link appropriate, or should I just use the client relation? Gee, in C I would declare a global variable here, but what can I do in a language that does not have global variables? How do I best integrate this piece of existing software into my design? Am I overusing multiple inheritance for this class? Should I use a multi-branch instruction or rely on dynamic binding? This structure does not look like anything we saw in class, but is it OK anyway?

The first iteration can teach students the solutions. In the second session, they will understand what the problems were.

SECOND-LEVEL COURSES

After the initial training, taken once or twice, some more courses may be useful. Here is a sampling of titles for such courses, each with an estimate of the duration:

- *Using the Base libraries* (2-3 days).

- *Using graphical libraries* (2-3 days).

- *Intermediate O-O design techniques* (2 days).

- *Advanced O-O design techniques* (2 days).

- *Mastering inheritance techniques* (2 days).

- *GUI* (Graphical User Interface) *development* (2-3 days).

- *Object-oriented analysis techniques with case studies* (3 days).

- *Interfacing objects with databases* (2 days).

- *Configuration management for object-oriented software* (1 day).

• *Designing libraries of reusable components*, with a case study. (This course should focus on a technical area relevant to the company's work, and falls somewhere between training and consulting.)

These titles are only examples, and most companies will need only a subset of the courses. Not all courses need be taken by all developers.

TRAINING THE MANAGERS

The above courses, introductory or more advanced, were meant for technical developers. If your organization is seriously considering the use of object-oriented techniques, you must also train the managers.

Two kinds of session will be useful here: courses for project managers; and courses for other managers, in particular senior executives, who will not lead projects themselves but whose views and decisions will affect projects that may use object-oriented development.

Consider the second category first. It is essential to involve higher management in the training. (If you have a budget for two courses only, one of them should be a course for the senior managers.) These will not be very long sessions; senior executives do not have much time anyway — being busy is part of the job description. But even a one-day awareness seminar will go a long way towards ensuring that the technology is introduced in the right way, and expectations properly set. The topics should be some of what this book covers, for example:

• The benefits: what to expect, and what not to expect.

• Effect on quality and productivity.

• Effect on the software process.

• Role of reuse.

Project leaders will need specific training too. They must of course be familiar with the basics of the technology; for this they can share some of the training with the developers. A course on the topic "*Managing object-oriented projects*" is also appropriate.

CHOOSING TRAINERS AND CONSULTANTS

There are now many companies offering object-oriented training, and also many consultants in the field. Any organization will have its own criteria for selecting the offerings that suit it best. But general advice can be given in the form of two rules.

The first rule helps make sure you get your money's worth:

OBJECT-ORIENTED RESPONSIBILITY PRINCIPLE

Never hire an object-oriented consultant who will only accept to consult for the analysis and design phases, or a trainer who will only take care of teaching analysis and design.

Unfortunately, you will find many consultants and trainers that refuse to stay on for the implementation phase. Usually the excuse takes the form of grandstanding: the person's or company's time is really too precious, and their competence too high, to be wasted on trifling details of implementation. What? Me, program?

Do not believe a word of this, and look elsewhere for help. Even if you are in the market for an analysis course, you will want trainers that offer the rest of the curriculum as well; and even for help at the analysis level only, you want consultants who, if asked to, are ready to continue all the way down to implementation.

Why is the Object-Oriented Responsibility Principle so important? The reason is that you need people who are willing to stand for the result of their work. Someone who does only analysis has an all too easy role: one can produce a stunning analysis document with hundreds or thousands of pretty-looking bubbles and arrows, use it to impress a lot of people (at least a lot of non-programmers), and get paid handsomely. But it is very difficult at that stage to know how good the result really is. The only significant test, as noted, is a successful implementation. Only when developers grapple with the task of building a working software product will you know whether the analysis was any good. So if you are hiring people to help you with the analysis you must make sure that they are prepared to stay around when the value of their contribution gets really put to the test. Strategists who run away at the first sign of enemy fire will not help you win the battle.

In a recent column in the *Los Angeles Times*, the president of MIT was lamenting that social values have become perverted in the US, with all the bright students wanting to become lawyers — lots of rewards, little risk — rather than engineers. Since the place of lawyers in society is not part of the topics of this book, we do not need to discuss the merits of such a complaint. But it definitely helps explain why, when in the mid-eighties object technology started reaching beyond its original circle, so many consultants all of a sudden discovered the true vocation of their lives: object-oriented analysis — all fun, no trouble; all sizzle, no steak; the bubbles and arrows of outrageous fortune.

> It actually happened in two stages. First there was a brief time of panic: when it seemed that object technology was about programming, a number of analysis consultants, worried that they might be forced to go back to real work, went on the offensive against the method, using elaborate technical arguments to show that it was flawed. But then a miracle occurred: someone came up with the idea of object-oriented analysis — spelling relief, and a return to business as usual.

What is wrong here is not object-oriented analysis, or doing consulting and training in this important area, but the idea of refusing to take any responsibility for the rest of the software process.

This could be called the Casanova stance. To simplify a bit, the first half — the first thousand pages — of the memoirs of Giacomo or Jacques Casanova, Chevalier of Steingalt, cover Casanova's youth in the seventeen-forties, his travels throughout Europe, and his adventures with numerous young women, some of whom entrusted to his care by their unsuspecting fathers. The second thousand pages show him going through many of the same cities in the seventeen-sixties, meeting not just his former friends but also their handsome children — who, often enough, look stunningly like him. It is a delightful book, although not the most moral one, as it is generally held now as then that someone who fathers children should also take some responsibility for them.

A modern manager who hires analysis-only (or analysis-and-design only) consultants or trainers for his project acts as an eighteenth-century father who engages Jacques Casanova as a preceptor to his only daughter.

This discussion highlights once again the place of analysis and design in object technology, so different from their role in earlier approaches. Many consultants and their clients, and much of the O-O analysis and design literature, still follow the pre-object paradigm, repainted with object colors: a waterfall-like view that considers analysis and design as separate, self-contained steps, meant to produce documents that will serve as a basis for the following steps. With those earlier approaches the consultants would help their customers do, for example, "structured analysis" and "structured design", and then let someone else handle the implementation. Now they expect to be doing "object-oriented analysis and design" and then run away (like Casanova when he left Venice for Corfu in May of 1744) while someone else takes care of the lowly task of actually producing running software.

At best this approach might yield better analysis and design documents; but however you look at it it is not object technology. Object technology implies seamlessness; it implies departing from the waterfall model and moving to a continuous software process in which software is built by successive iterations of the same document; it even implies, as we saw in an earlier chapter, the disappearance of any clear-cut difference between design and implementation. That is why you want your trainers and consultants, including those who specialize in the early tasks of the software process, to master the rest of that process too, and to be prepared, if you ask them, to continue working on the consequences of their advice.

The second rule for choosing trainers and consultants will help apply the right selection criteria. With the explosion of interest in the object-oriented method it is not surprising that many people now claim to be experts in the field. You will need to sort out these claims to select the people who are best prepared to help you.

The usual criteria will apply: how impressive the person's or company's résumé is; education; previous participation in similar applications; breadth of experience; demonstrated understanding of the technology; mix of management and technical expertise; references provided by previous customers; your personal rapport with the candidates; articles published, books, talks at conferences.

All this is useful here as it would be when you hire consultants and trainers in any technical area. But there is something special about expertise in the object-oriented field:

OBJECT-ORIENTED EXPERTISE PRINCIPLE

No one is an expert in object technology who has not played a major role in the development of a successful object-oriented library of reusable software components.

Reusable software construction is the achievement that, more than anything else, distinguishes the object-oriented method from anything before it. Until you have built a successful library you cannot claim to be an authority in the field.

"Successful" here means actually reused on a broad scale, by teams far removed from the original library builders. The discussion of reusability (see "LEVELS OF MODULE REUSABILITY, page 118) will distinguish four levels of reusability for a component; the expression "a successful object-oriented library", as used in the Object-Oriented Expertise Principle, denotes a library that has reached level 4, at which it must have been used in systems produced by people that have no direct contact with the authors.

The Object-Oriented Expertise Principle will make your life easier; as you start applying it, the pool of candidates will quickly shrink.

REUSABILITY CONSULTANTS

The topic of consultants suggests another observation. Companies that undertake object-oriented projects may need to use consultants in the usual ways: technical tasks such as analysis, design and implementation; management consulting.

But there is also another, more novel use for consultants, at least those who satisfy the Object-Oriented Expertise Principle. If you are serious about reuse and interested in developing your own reusable software (that is to say, ready to move to what the discussion of this topic in chapter 5 will call the *producer's view* of reusability), then you can rely on the reusability competence of object-oriented consultants to help you produce your own components.

This scheme can yield a fruitful collaboration between a group that has the application domain expertise (your group) and another that has application-independent expertise in building reusable software — the consultants.

PILOT PROJECTS

A company that is considering adopting object technology on a more or less broad scale will usually want to try it first on a few selected projects — the pilot projects. What is the best way to select and plan the pilot projects?

The usual advice is to avoid choosing something too big, based on the risk argument: avoiding to bet the house on new ideas. But you should also look at the other side of the issue. If you choose a pilot project that is too small, the risk is not what happens if it fails; in fact, for a small enough project, you may succeed with *any* approach. The risk is what happens in case of success: the pilot project and its success may not teach you anything. You will not know whether the success is due to the technology that you are trying, or to the small size of the problem.

A pilot project must teach you something. Hence the rule:

> **THE PILOT PROJECT PRINCIPLE**
>
> If you are using an example project to evaluate object technology, choose a project whose potential results will be useful to the company, so that its success or failure will be felt.

For success to mean anything, you must be prepared to take the risk of failure. Not every company is ready to take this risk. If you are not, it is better *not* to undertake a pilot project now; a risk-free project would not be meaningful enough. In such a case it is better to avoid wasting any money or resources on the pilot project; wait for whatever time it takes to change the circumstances and make your company object-aware enough to undertake a serious effort.

The Pilot Project Principle has another justification. A pilot project is not just meant to ascertain success or failure. Of course if you have reached a stage at which you are willing to devote resources to such a project you must have a feeling that object technology can work for you, and you expect success. You need to test this prediction, but you will want the project to yield more than a yes or no answer. If it does succeed it should help you understand *how* to use object technology; it should set a *precedent*; and it will show an *example* that will entice other projects to follow the same path. These are further reasons for selecting a significant project. The project should produce results that the company needs, so as to catch the attention of other groups and make them want to profit from the same benefits. This may be stated as a corollary to the Pilot Project Principle:

> ## THE KILLER APP PRINCIPLE
>
> For a pilot project, select, if possible, a project whose results will provide new and highly visible services to the corporation.

"Killer App" (for Application) is programmerese for a system which no one has done before and which will dazzle everyone. The observation behind the Killer App Principle is well known to anyone who has been responsible for pushing software methods or ideas in a company: although it is all right to preach, the best way to convince people is still to show them miracles. By preaching you can win over a few apostles (a dozen or so, according to some studies, seems to be a typical success rate); but perform a few miracles and your following will grow much faster.

Sometimes a Killer App can be quite modest. A long time ago, while trying to promote modern software engineering techniques in a large company, I wrote, for circumstantial reasons, an efficient sorting routine, and put it into the company's library. To a recent computing science graduate, this was a one-hour effort — applying second-year CS techniques — and I did not think much about it. I was stunned to see how much it impressed the programming staff: having had little formal computing science training, they were used to techniques that would sort an array of n elements in time proportional to n^2, whereas mine used $n \log (n)$ time, as I had been taught. On large arrays the difference is tremendous; my little exercise meant that some problems previously thought intractable were now becoming routine! But the most interesting consequence was that afterwards many people who until then had paid no attention to my exhortations about programming methodology started to listen quite carefully. I had shown that I was capable not just of giving advice (the most common ability in the world) but also of *doing things they could not do*.

The lesson is, I think, a general one. To succeed, consultants, advisors and technology champions ("evangelists" as Apple Computer calls them) should do more than consult, advise, champion and evangelize. They should use the power of example to show directly what can be done. More generally, whenever you preach *methods* you should also teach *techniques*.

A FAILURE

To illustrate the problems associated with pilot projects, it is useful to look at two examples. The first is a failure; the second (discussed in the next section) is a success. Both projects have been described in the literature; both used Eiffel, so that the comparison is meaningful.

The failure was a large project at Cognos, documented in a number of presentations by Burton Leathers of Cognos and his article in *SOOPS: Symposium on Object-Oriented Programming Emphasizing Practical Applications*, Marist College, Poughkeepsie, New York, 14-15 September 1990, pages 66 to 80. Cognos is a Canadian software house which around 1988 decided to replace part of its existing technology by a newly designed object-oriented product. The experience reads like a case study about how not to manage a software project:

- In a few weeks the company went from a handful of O-O gurus to more than 120 object-oriented developers.

- In spite of the magnitude of the project and the novelty of the technology (this was 1989) no consulting was ever sought from the O-O vendor, and no training except for a two-day session late in the project.

- Instead of using the standard version of the O-O tools, Cognos decided to obtain a source license and start modifying them. Quoting Burton Leathers: *The availability of the compiler source and the presence of some very capable compiler people* [Cognos had previously tried to develop its own O-O language, and failed] *led us to make changes to the compiler because it was easier than having* [the vendor] *make them. This was a terrible trap.* Indeed it was: after a few weeks it made it impossible for the vendor to provide technical support! In addition it also made it impossible after a while to let Cognos benefit from updates to a technology which at the time was still quickly evolving.

- Management expectations were not properly set.

- The commitment to object technology, initiated the technical people, was accepted by upper management, but did not have an upper-management champion.

- Goals were unrealistic. Quoting again from Burton Leathers's article: *In the "Mythical Man-Month", Brooks notes that [...] nine women cannot produce a child in a month. This did not deter management at Cognos from attempting the software engineering equivalent. By setting an unjustifiable final delivery date, management were obliged to create schedules which had inherently serial activities proceeding in parallel. It was this schedule telescoping which meant that the debugger was completed after the bulk of the code had been created and the source control and configuration management tools and procedures were not in place until long after they were desperately needed.*

It is hard to think of how one could have accumulated more management mistakes in a single project. Yet development was proceeding. The inevitable happened, however: concerned that the new product was not advancing fast enough, and that the old one was losing market share, the company's higher management decided to cancel the advanced project and to bring developers back to improving the old product.

This example has often been quoted as an argument against object technology, or Eiffel, or both. But to anyone who reads Leathers's article the conclusion will be obvious: the failure had little to do with technical issues; it was one of management and planning.

The lesson of the Cognos experience is clear:

> ## O-O SOFTWARE ENGINEERING PRINCIPLE
>
> Using object-oriented techniques and an object-oriented language is not a substitute for good project management and the application of software engineering principles.

A SUCCESS STORY

From the Cognos case it might seem that the best approach to implementing object technology is prudence and patience.

This would be a wrong inference. Although some companies will prefer to go slowly, for others a fast, bold, well-planned move to object orientation may be a unique opportunity to gain a decisive edge over their competition. The Bytex case provides a good illustration.

The following discussion of the Bytex project is primarily based on an interview of Roger Osmond, the project manager, by Rock Howard in *Eiffel Outlook*, vol. 2, no. 4, Nov.-Dec. 1992. Some elements have also been taken from talks given by Mr. Osmond at several TOOLS conferences (Technology of Object-Oriented Languages and Systems).

Bytex is a Westboro (Massachusetts) company providing advanced networking solutions specializing in "hubs" that connect local area networks — a multi-billion-dollar market. In late 1989 Bytex, then primarily a provider of electronic matrix switches for wide area networks, found itself in a difficult situation. The difficulty was not market share, since Bytex was the principal player in its field, doing a little under $40 million annually, and continuing to increase its dominance; it was the market itself. It is not too hard to guess that a company focusing in 1989 on networking for mainframe computers did not show exciting growth prospects. The risk existed of slowly becoming a $0 million company.

It seemed more desirable to become a $80-million company quickly. But how? Clearly the competition had not waited. Some bold move was required.

Bytex decided to build a new workstation-oriented system: an "Intelligent Switching System", based on a "smart hub" that allows a network manager to set up multiple Local Area Networks within a single hub. The major competitive advantage of this solution is that a customer who changes a network configuration — and customers tend to change configurations all the time! — does not need to perform any physical re-wiring: the reconfiguration will entirely be done under software control. The time and effort saved by not having to re-wire cables is an enormous benefit for the customer. This approach also enhances network reliability and availability because the least reliable components of the network, the cables and their connectors, become inert — once wired, they do not need to be manipulated again.

Because of the time pressure, the quality requirements and the complexity of the job, Bytex decided to use object technology. There was little object experience in the company; conventional wisdom might have suggested a phased approach, with successive pilot projects of increasing scale. Instead, the company moved fast. But in contrast with the Cognos case the project was carefully planned and prepared. Independent consultants were brought from the outside to help select a language and tools. Once the selection was made, the Bytex team received the proper training. Then they went ahead.

The result: in 1991 Bytex began shipping the new product. In the following years sales of that product doubled each year, and moved beyond what the core product had yielded at its peak. Bytex has since been involved in two significant mergers, making it part first of a $220-million company and then of a $2-billion one. Its technical leadership and ability to deliver ambitious, quality products were key ingredients to these mergers.

As to the original project, the Series 7700 Intelligent Switching System: the 7700 was named "Product of the Year" by *LAN Magazine;* it was chosen as a "Hot Product" in the LAN area for *Data Communications* magazine; the same magazine gave it its Tester's Choice Award in 1993.

As the product was being prepared, object-oriented ideas played a key role in bringing it to market quickly and responding to customer demand. When a pre-release was unveiled in March 1991, interest from customers was favorable but included many suggestions for additional capabilities. Object technology allowed the developers to add significant new features in cycles of as little as 4 to 6 weeks, impressing customers as well as the marketing and sales departments with the responsiveness of Engineering.

After the first official release in the Fall of 1991, updates continued at a regular rate, all made possible by the flexibility of the product's object-oriented architecture: support for six new card types, a new hub type, Token Ring monitoring capability, and many others.

Like many similar projects, the development had to interface with existing C code, but the technique of keeping the O-O and C parts separate and communicating through official interfaces was preferable to that of using a C extension. In the interview, published a year and a half after the first official release, Osmond noted the importance of choosing a pure rather than hybrid approach to object-oriented software construction: *"If Bytex had chosen C++ for this project the development team would still be coding for the first release"*.

A study of the article reveals interesting differences with the Cognos case. The project started with half a dozen software engineers and grew only to slightly over a dozen: in other words Bytex avoided inflating the team. Also, the project was started on the initiative of the then Vice President of Engineering (Dr. Michael Mancusi, now General Manager of Bytex), who *"played the key role of Product Champion and convinced upper management to back the project* [...] *Management commitment for OOT was an implicit part of the project from the beginning"*. This helped set the expectations right. Another supporter in higher management was Joseph E. Massery, then Director of Software Engineering (now Vice President of Engineering). In fact, although Roger Osmond notes that there were some unrealistic expectations, one of his slides at the TOOLS USA 94 conference read:

> **OOP holds *MORE* promise
> than the current hype would have us believe.**

Here are some of the lessons of the Bytex project:

• Although not a substitute for good software engineering practices (as stated above by the O-O Software Engineering Principle), object technology can, for a team applying these practices, make the difference between commercial success and failure.

• It is also essential to know what you expect from object orientation. (The questionnaire given at the beginning of this chapter and discussed at the end should help.)

• One of the main contributions of the technology, when applied well, is the flexibility of the resulting software architectures, which in a highly competitive market can give a company the edge by enabling it to provide extremely fast response to strategic customer requirements.

• Management awareness and support is crucial. This last advice, highlighted by the difference between our two case studies, yields a principle of its own:

> **MANAGEMENT CHAMPION PRINCIPLE**
>
> Before undertaking object-oriented development on any significant scale, be sure to have a committed champion in upper management, who understands the intent and scope of the technology.

If you are promoting object technology into your company, it is your responsibility to teach upper management about its "intent and scope", emphasizing in particular that its major contribution affects quality more than short-term productivity improvements.

The Bytex example also holds a lesson about the proper pace of moving to object technology. Although conventional wisdom suggests going slowly, fortune will smile to the competent bold.

CHOOSING THE RIGHT PEOPLE

For the pilot projects, and later for others that will use object-oriented techniques, you will need to be careful about team selection. Here is a list of desirable qualities:

> **THE IDEAL O-O DEVELOPER PROFILE**
>
> • Ability to abstract.
> • Ability to adapt to new modes of thinking.
> • Well organized.
> • Experience with as many areas of computing as possible.
> • Experience with as many approaches to computing — programming languages, software development methods — as possible.
> • Experience at all levels of the software process: analysis (specification), design, implementation, maintenance.

You will want people who have a strong *ability to abstract*. Object technology, as noted several times already, is not about objects but about abstraction. You need people who are able to see the concept behind the examples, the general behind the specific, the essential behind the auxiliary.

You need team members who can *adapt to new modes of thinking*. Object technology makes it possible, in a very flexible way, to encapsulate reasoning patterns into software schemes. Those who apply it should be able to learn new patterns fast.

They should also be *well organized*. Object-oriented development relies on systematic techniques and multi-person collaboration through standardized interfaces. We want excellent software developers, but not of the "lone and messy genius" type.

Look for people with *experience in many areas*. The gods of objects will smile upon the person who can spot the recurrence of patterns encountered in previous work. Object technology is the quintessential **generalist** approach, where barriers between areas of specialization fall. As usual, you will need experts in individual fields (in fact, the technology helps them refine and apply their expertise); but you do not want narrow-minded programmers who have only heard about one area of development.

The quest for generalists means that you should be looking for team members having *experience with many approaches to computing*. The object-oriented method is the cuckoo of the software world, always ready to deposit its eggs into another bird's nest. If you identify a useful mode of computing, often from another approach or area — functional programming à la Lisp, Logic programming à la Prolog, database programming, entity-relationship modeling — you can write O-O classes that will encapsulate that mode and apply it to your developments. To benefit from this versatility of the method, you should look for people who already know as many of these approaches as possible.

Finally, the seamless character of O-O development, one of the *leitmotive* of this book, should be a major boost to your projects. This means that you will have little use for analysts (specifiers) who cannot design or code, or for coders who cannot do design or analysis. You need people who have *experience at all levels of the software process* and whom you can solicit for all the intertwined activities of the cluster lifecycle. Here too you are not rejecting experts: some people will give their truly outstanding performances at the specification stage, others are brilliant at implementation. But all should be familiar with the entire process, and be able to help at every step.

The theme of the last few items of advice was the same: we want generalists, not narrow-minded specialists. As noted, expertise in specific areas is of course precious, but it must not come at the expense of mastery of the big picture. The team members must possess a broad set of skills. This changeover from specialists to generalists is actually a larger trend, affecting many industries and spotted in a recent influential article in *The Economist*.

TECHNOLOGY EVOLUTION AND PEOPLE

How do the above requirements affect the evolution of the software profession? A comparison with other technological changes will help understand the answer.

One of the aims of moving to object technology is to increase productivity; in plain English, this means doing more and better work with fewer people.

The history of technology shows two kinds of productivity advance. In both kinds, some jobs are rendered obsolete; automation does not really mean that we replace people with machines, rather that we replace people who did a certain job with other people who operate machines doing that job (or more commonly a different job replacing the earlier one). The two kinds of advance differ in the nature of the new jobs:

1 • In cases of the first kind, the new jobs require less qualification than the old ones. This happens when a technology evolution makes a whole set of skills useless, so that the replacement tools can be operated by people without the extensive training and experience that were previously required. The evolution of the automobile industry, and of other transportation industries before it, contains many examples of this kind. More recently, Computer-Aided Design tools have all but eliminated the need for professional draftsmen.

2 • In cases of the second kind, the new jobs require *more* qualification than the old. There is still an economical advantage to the move, however, since even though the new specialists are usually paid more there will be far fewer of them. The evolution of farming in industrialized countries is typical of this category.

Changes brought about by object technology are of the second type. Expect to need fewer people — this is the productivity gain — but with a higher average qualification.

Some situations may seem to belong to case 1; for example, much of the expertise gained in older methods, languages and operating systems may suddenly become unneeded. But such expertise often involved knowledge that was rather low-level, although sometimes very detailed. Not so long go, for example, trade magazines carried many job offers for programmers fluent in IBM's OS 360 Job Control Language; who is hiring JCL programmers today?

ELITISM?

A certain tone of elitism may seem to resonate from the previous comments. This is a possible criticism, and it must be addressed.

First, we are not requiring geniuses. The qualities that we seek are largely about openness, flexibility, ability to reason at a high level of abstraction, willingness to learn new thought patterns. These are skills that can be nurtured. Indeed in ISE's experience one of the rewards of having taught object-oriented ideas to so many people for many years and in many different environments has been to discover that individuals with extremely diverse backgrounds can become O-O masters. In our practice they have included software developers with computing science degrees from world-class universities, but also PhDs in theoretical physics, as well as old-time COBOL, FORTRAN or even BASIC programmers, self-trained software developers with little formal education, and former managers who late in their careers discovered the beauties of technical work.

Differences in technical abilities will remain, however; in fact software development seems to exacerbate them. Numerous studies have confirmed what every software manager knows informally: that individual differences between programmers are huge. It is not uncommon to see one person succeed where eight had previously failed. Some published studies show ratios of 20 to 1 in programmer capability, between people of similar backgrounds occupying similar positions in the same organization.

Software managers, naturally, will try to use the people that are at the higher end of this scale.

How does object technology affect this discussion? Here too we can relate the discussion to a more general distinction in the history of technological advances, with two cases that parallel the ones introduced in the preceding section:

1 • In some cases, a technology breakthrough reduces differences between individual practitioners of the trade, enabling everyone to handle tasks that were previously reserved for the best experts. To take a low-tech example, anyone that has a good washing machine can now produce results that only the best domestics could achieve, with much effort, in less automated times. Another example is computerized taxi dispatching; on a recent trip to Paris, an experienced taxi driver whom I was complimenting on his fancy on-board computer system went into a bitter complaint of how this had ruined the business: what with every newcomer being now in the same league as the old-timer who previously could get the best business by relying on long-accumulated knowledge about the fastest routes, arrival patterns in railway stations, and likely times of traffic congestion.

2 • In other instances, however, the advance has the inverse effect — providing the best experts with ways to increase their existing advantage. The ethnographer Claude Lévi-Strauss tells of introducing writing to an Amazonian tribe; the chief immediately saw the benefits of this invention and confiscated it for his exclusive use, as a way to reinforce his power.

Object technology can make everyone more effective, and as such can benefit the most qualified developers as well as the least qualified ones. But it does not benefit everyone equally. This is the kind of technology advance that, like writing for Amazonians, tends to help most those who are *already* at the forefront. Give object-oriented computing to an average programmer, and the programmer will become a little better. Give it to a top programmer, and the results may be a superb improvement in quality and productivity. Everyone gets better; but some get more better than others.

One may complain that this is unfair; but then life is unfair. And we should not forget that the primary aim of software development is not to make life easy for software developers, but to satisfy the users (and potential victims) of the resulting software.

In a panel at a Unix conference, responding to someone who complained that object technology is readily picked by the best developers who use it to their advantage, but can leave others behind, Bill Joy (the designer of Berkeley Unix and cofounder of Sun Microsystems, who is known for speaking his mind) retorted: "Good! Then at least the software will be written by the good programmers". This is right to the point. Software quality and productivity are not just the pet peeves of technical perfectionists: they hold the key to customer satisfaction, and in many cases to the protection of human property and human safety.

The issue remains of how best to employ people other than the top software developers; it will be discussed later in this chapter (see "WHAT TO DO WITH THE OTHERS?", page 95). Important as its social consequences may be, however, it must leave precedence to the fundamental issue of software engineering: how to produce the best possible software in the best possible way.

TWO CAVEATS

The advice given so far about how to select people for object-oriented projects was centered on positive characteristics. Some negative advice (about whom *not* to hire) must also be included.

The first one addresses a particular type of background. As noted above, it is not possible to specify a single profile that would be required for object success, and software developers with widely different work experience, not necessarily the most prestigious, have turned out to be excellent O-O developers. But one special category justifies a cautious attitude if you are hiring people for an O-O project:

> **PRUDENT HIRING PRINCIPLE**
>
> Beware of C hackers.

A "C hacker" is someone who has had too much practice of writing low-level C software and making use of all the special techniques and tricks permitted by that language.

Why single out C? First, interestingly enough, one seldom hears about Pascal hackers, Ada hackers or Modula hackers. C, which since the late nineteen-seventies has spread rapidly throughout the computing community, especially in the USA, typifies a theology of computing where the Computer is the central deity and its altar reads Efficiency. Everything is sacrificed to low-level performance, and programs are built in terms of addresses, words, memory cells, pointers, manual memory allocation and deallocation, unsafe type conversions, signals and similar machine-oriented constructs. In this almost monotheist cult, where the Microsecond and the Kilobyte complete the trinity, there is little room for such idols of software engineering as Readability, Provability and Extendibility.

Not surprisingly, former believers need a serious debriefing before they can rejoin the rest of the computing community and its progress towards more modern forms of software development.

The above principle does not say "Stay away from C hackers", which would show lack of faith in the human aptitude to betterment. There have indeed been cases of former C hackers who became born-again O-O developers. But in general you should be cautious about including C hackers in your projects, as they are often the ones who have the most trouble adapting to the abstraction-based form of software development that object technology embodies.

The second rule addresses a general issue rather than a specific category of people:

> **"FEWER MAY BE BETTER" PRINCIPLE OF HIRING FOR OBJECT-ORIENTED PROJECTS**
>
> When in doubt, abstain.

Like the preceding one, this principle is not an absolute rule but a guideline to be applied with moderation (otherwise, you could use it repetitively to bring down the number of project participants to zero, not a very useful result). But it does state an important observation: in staffing a project, especially at the beginning, and especially with a new and ambitious technology, bigger is not necessarily better.

According to a recent *New York Times* article that reported on a study of couples over a long period, the originally less intelligent or cultivated partner in a marriage tends, along the way, to reach the level of the other. Whether this assertion is indeed true for marriages will be left for other authors to decide; but in my experience it seldom applies to software projects. What seems more applicable there is the Bad Apple theory: one person can damage the whole project by slowing others down, asking them frequent questions that detract them from their own priorities, producing software that will later be found inadequate and will have to be redone, or infecting the rest of the group with contagious non-enthusiasm.

The consequence for the manager is that you should refrain from adding people who are not essential or not at the right level. This rule is especially applicable to your first O-O projects, and to the **initial stages** of all projects, where it is especially crucial to ensure consistency and solidity of the overall design. Within a project, the same rule applies to individual clusters: to start a good broth, use few cooks.

> The chapter on the role of managers will come back to these issues, discussing in particular why it may be necessary, when attempting to rescue a troubled project, to remove people (see "CRISIS REMEDY", page 133).

Some circumstances justify taking a less strict attitude. If at some advanced stage of a successful project you notice that certain extra functionalities, of which no one in the team has the time to take care, would make the end product more attractive, then it may be reasonable to add a few people, possibly less experienced, to the team. This assumes that the project is well under control; that it is already meeting or poised to meet its essential requirements; that the new functionalities can be implemented without too much interaction with the rest of the development; and that it would not be a catastrophe to ship the product without these functionalities.

In all other cases, and especially at the beginning of a project or cluster, you should be very wary of making the group bigger. As Brooks noted many years ago, the number of potential interactions in a group of size n grows not as n but as n^2. It is surprising how much you can achieve with a group of 4 to 10 talented, enthusiastic object-oriented developers. And if the developers are not enthusiastic or not talented, using more of them is not going to help.

As a rule of thumb, a pilot project — if it is really a pilot project, rather than a development such as the Bytex example which is a major corporate endeavor but happens to be the first significant one in the company to use object-oriented techniques — should not need more than half a dozen developers. (This was actually the Bytex project size for many months.) At the other end of the spectrum, it is a rare object-oriented effort that needs more than twenty developers; such projects do exist, of course, but they should not be undertaken lightly:

LARGE O-O PROJECT PRINCIPLE

No company should undertake an object-oriented project involving more than 12 developers except under the following conditions:

- In-depth mastery of the object-oriented method (preferably backed by previous successful projects).
- Availability of excellent project management expertise.
- Adherence to strict and clearly specified software engineering practices.

One may object that these requirements should apply to all projects, above or below 12 developers. But a dozen people seems to be the approximate limit beyond which it is simply impossible to survive without them.

The good news is that with a team of that size made of competent and enthusiastic O-O developers, a good O-O language, a good O-O environment, sound software engineering practices, and a good manager, you can quickly achieve results that more traditional approaches could not even dream of, even with a team many times as big.

SOFTWARE QUALIFICATIONS AND THEIR EVOLUTION

The observations made earlier in this chapter on elitism and the role of technology changes in software suggest a reflection on the evolution of the software profession.

In spite of appearances, the observation that we will need more qualified people does not contradict the often advertized *"move to end-user computing"*. Object-oriented ideas are indeed at the forefront of the methods that make it possible to give "end-users" (that is to say, people who rely on software systems but are not computing professionals) more power to control and adapt the systems that they use. But every time we lower the requirements on end-users of our systems, we must raise the requirements on the authors of these systems, as expressed by the following rule:

EASE-OF-USE PRINCIPLE

An easier-to-use system is harder-to-design.

This rule also reflects the evolution of the software profession, which is no longer a single occupation but rather a spectrum of competence levels.

Twenty-five years ago, being able to program a computer in, say, FORTRAN or COBOL, was a professional qualification sufficient to land you a job. Not any more. Nowadays many an eighteen-year old with a personal computer at home has logged in as many hours of programming, or some form of it, as a professional programmer used to do in the first few years of a career.

Instead of the old situation what we now see, as illustrated by the figure, is a whole range of degrees of competence:

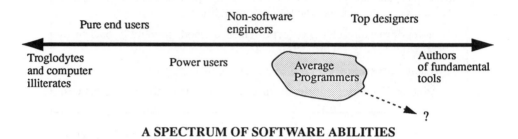

A SPECTRUM OF SOFTWARE ABILITIES

The category at the far left covers the rapidly dwindling part of the population that does not use computers. Continuing from left to right, a *pure end-user* is someone who uses the computer and the programs it runs as mere tools, with little idea of how the computer works and no influence over what the programs do. Next, *power users* are able to change the behavior of their software. They usually started out as pure end-users, but curiosity led them to lift the hood and find out what was going on inside; they often know more about programming than what a typical "professional" programmer did in 1970. (In the same way, a science-inclined high-school student knows more mathematics and physics, in some areas at least, than Descartes, Pascal or Newton.) Then we find those engineers from other disciplines who are not computing scientists by training or job description but are sometimes programmers by the reality of their day-to-day work. The next category includes "average" programmers, who can produce code in a programming language, sometimes several, but have not been involved in high-level design or system architecture. Then the best designers. Finally, the software equivalent of chip designers in the hardware industry: the people who write the building blocks on which everyone else relies — operating systems, networking software, compilers, general-purpose libraries of reusable software components. The competence requirements that are (or should be) imposed on this last group of software professionals are commensurate with the trouble that will ensue if they leave a deficiency in any one of their products.

The evolution of the software industry raises a major problem for the middle categories and in particular for the one labeled "Average Programmers", which the figure shows highlighted and with a question mark hanging over its future. As the industry progresses, this group will increasingly be under attack from both left and right. Progress in basic tools and reusable components means that many tasks that previously required a programmer can now be addressed by using general-purpose tools or assembling reusable components. Combined with the increased role of computing in general education and the wide availability of personal computers, this also implies that more and more of the programmers' tasks can be handled by nonprofessionals — the people to the left of the Average programmers on the figure.

Although some of this evolution would have occurred anyway, object technology accelerates and reinforces it. Like the industrial revolution of the eighteenth and nineteenth centuries, it is not so much harming workers as favoring certain categories of workers over others.

Here the threatened group is the middle one, Average Programmers. The technology helps the groups on both the left and right parts of the figure: it enables the people on the right (the most competent software specialists) to produce ever more powerful tools and components that will enable the people on the left (non-computing professionals) to solve many problems that previously required professional programmers. Because of the Ease-of-Use Principle, the advanced groups on the right need not worry about the rise of end-user computing: to build products that will give ever more power to ever less computing-savvy users, we need ever more expert specialists. But this is all to the detriment of the Average Programmers, who will find themselves sandwiched between users with increasingly sophisticated tools and experts with increasingly valuable skills.

The concrete short-term inference, for a manager, is that you should aim for the best software people in your organization.

Actually this should not be too difficult. Object technology naturally attracts the best software developers; they will besiege you to let them join the project.

FOSTERING A GRASSROOTS PHENOMENON

The last comment will have reminded you — as a good manager you definitely know this — that a technology change such as the move to object orientation cannot be fully imposed from the top. Even if the initial impulse comes from higher management, success can only come if the people most affected by the change commandeer the technology and transform the original top-down initiative into a bottom-up movement.

Knowing how to produce such a reversal is part of standard managerial skills. In the case of object technology, this will be made easier by the attraction that this technique holds for the most competent developers. It is interesting to see how quickly such people embrace the ideas: you start showing object orientation to them, let them play a little with a good O-O environment, and they are hooked for the rest of their lives. Never will they want to go back to anything else.

The pilot projects should take advantage of this phenomenon by relying on a combination of the best technology — the O-O method with a shining language and environment to support it — and the most enthusiastic and competent people. This explosive cocktail can start the reengineering of the software process of your company — and lead you to Object Success.

WHAT TO DO WITH THE OTHERS?

As noted above, the relatively high requirements defined for object-oriented developers do not mean we are looking for geniuses. Many people will be able to make the transition.

But, let us face it, as with any significant technical evolution some people will just not follow. What should you do with them?

The question comes up regularly in industry forums. I once heard from Adele Goldberg of Smalltalk fame (at a panel at Object Expo at which we were both speaking, in New York in June of 1992) the suggestion of using the less object-literate people as testers for the work of the best object-oriented developers.

This idea makes me uneasy: would we use the less advanced engineers, in a nuclear plant or aircraft factory, as safety engineers? In software like elsewhere, quality assurance (done in particular at the "Validation & Verification" step of the cluster model) is a crucial task; it is meant to ensure that the software satisfies all quality requirements: that it is bug-free, efficient, easy to use, consistent with user expectations. Such a job clearly requires people at the highest level of expertise.

The problem arises out of conflicting social pressures, pitting the needs of a business's longtime employees against those of its shareholders and customers. As such it has no perfect solution, but one approach at least seems preferable to the one just mentioned. To understand it, consider again the pictorial illustration of the scale of available skills (page 94) and the evolution that it reflects.

For the rightmost part of the scale — the development of fundamental tools and mission-critical systems — what is needed is the most capable people, period. (Reusable software components, in particular, should be produced by the best developers.) Accusations of elitism do not weigh very much against the potential consequences of the reverse policy, which range from delivering sloppy products and displeasing customers to causing life-threatening accidents, as bad software can do. The primary goal of software development is not to provide employment to existing software staffs; it is to ensure that the systems that control many aspects of industrial societies, from air traffic control to mail-order business, will work correctly and efficiently. If a malfunction in your software kills someone or brings one of your customers to bankruptcy, the defense that you tried to be kind to the faithful veterans of your programming group will not help you much in court.

But with the switch to reuse-based software development we can in some cases at least have a job for the less expert people: assembling these top-quality components and combining them in various ways. To assemble components, one needs to understand the essential aspects of the technology and to work on the basis of abstract interface descriptions; but the required skills are nowhere close to those it takes to *build* the components.

Here too object technology bring to the software world a phenomenon that has been apparent for many years in the hardware field: a division of labor between a relatively small number of leading-edge producers of basic components, and a larger group of engineers who essentially work on assembling systems from components produced by the first category.

This scheme seems to provide enough flexibility to accommodate the variety in levels of professionalism and depth of object-oriented expertise that characterizes the software community.

A SUMMARY OF TRANSITION PRINCIPLES

This chapter has given numerous pieces of advice meant to help the managers of companies that are considering moving to object technology, whether on a small scale or with high ambitions. It is useful to summarize these precepts in concise form. This is the purpose of the table which follows.

THE *OBJECT SUCCESS* RULES
FOR A HAPPY TRANSITION TO OBJECT TECHNOLOGY

- If you decide to use object orientation, even for trial purposes, apply the method all the way: from analysis to design, implementation and maintenance.
- To learn object-oriented software construction: Take the initial training courses. Then try your hand at object-oriented development. Then take the initial training courses.
- Train the managers, not just the developers.
- Never hire an object-oriented consultant who will only accept to consult for the analysis and design phases, or a trainer who will only accept to teach analysis and design.
- No one is an expert in object technology who has not played a major role in the development of a successful object-oriented library of reusable software components.
- If you are using an example project to evaluate object technology, choose a project whose results will be useful to the company, so that its success or failure will be felt.
- For a pilot project, select, if possible, a project whose results will provide new and highly visible services to the corporation.
- Using object-oriented techniques and an object-oriented language is not a substitute for good project management and the application of software engineering principles.
- Beware of C hackers.
- In hiring developers for O-O projects: When in doubt, abstain.
- Do not undertake an object-oriented project involving more than 12 developers except with: in-depth mastery of the method; availability of excellent project management expertise; adherence to strict and clearly specified software engineering practices.

APPENDIX: INTERPRETING THE QUESTIONNAIRE

The questionnaire that appeared at the beginning of this chapter is meant to help you understand your goals in moving to object technology, and find out where you are now, so that you can properly plan for the move and set proper expectations. The answers will also provide some guidance as to the kind of object-oriented environment that is most appropriate for your needs.

For convenience the questionnaire is reproduced in the next two pages.

The purpose of question 1 is to let you state what your aims are. There is more than one possible reason to be attracted to object technology. Many people will find the goals listed to be all desirable, but "All of the above" is not an option; you are requested to sort these goals in order of decreasing importance to you. In evaluating the answers, what will matter is the letters in brackets associated with your top choices.

If [A] dominates these choices, you are essentially driven by the search for

THE *OBJECT SUCCESS* QUESTIONNAIRE
(reproduced from pages 74-75)

1 What are your major goals in considering object technology?

Rate these reasons in order of decreasing value to you, starting with 1 for the most important. If one of them does not apply to your case, do not rate it. Before answering make sure you have read all the reasons listed. Disregard letters in brackets, such as [A].

[A]   1.1 __ Following the general evolution of the software industry.

[D]   1.2 __ Reducing maintenance costs.

[E]   1.3 __ Reducing debugging time.

[F]   1.4 __ Benefiting from external libraries of reusable components.

[B]   1.5 __ Benefiting from an advanced development environment.

[D]   1.6 __ Making the resulting software easier to modify.

[A]   1.7 __ Remaining compatible with the evolution of some of your business partners (such as customers, suppliers, hardware vendors, software houses).

[C]   1.8 __ Quickly producing partial experimental versions ("prototypes") of new products, to assess some of their properties before starting the final versions.

[F]   1.9 __ Capitalizing on your software efforts by making the results more reusable.

[B]   1.10 __ Improving time-to-market for new products.

[E]   1.11 __ Preventing the appearance of bugs.

[B]   1.12 __ Decreasing software development costs.

2 What is your company's current exposure to object technology?

Choose one (the highest number that applies):

2.0 - Novice level.

2.1 - Some people have general knowledge about object technology, but no one has had any significant practice.

2.2 - Some people have used object-like technology, for example by programming in Ada and using associated design techniques, in earlier projects — either within the company or elsewhere.

2.3 - Some people have used object technology in earlier projects that included implementation in an object-oriented language (not just analysis or design) but the company has not completed any such project.

2.4 - The company has successfully completed at least one small project (300 classes or less) using object-oriented techniques in an object-oriented language.

2.5 - The company has successfully completed at least one significant project (more than 300 classes), using object-oriented techniques, in a hybrid object-oriented language such as C++ or CLOS.

2.6 - The company has successfully completed at least one significant project (as defined above) in a pure object-oriented language such as Eiffel or Smalltalk.

THE *OBJECT SUCCESS* QUESTIONNAIRE
(continued)

2.7 - The company has been developing software using object-oriented techniques in a pure object-oriented language for two or more years, and has successfully completed a number of significant projects with it.

2.8 - Same as 2.7, but for five or more years.

3 What is your company's current software process?

3.1 - Does your company develop most of its software itself?

3.2 - Does your company subcontract most of its software to an outside source (software house, MIS department of the parent company)?

3.3 - Do you have a recommended software process model? (Circle one.)

    3.3.1 No standard process model.

    3.3.2 Waterfall or similar.

    3.3.3 Spiral.

    3.3.4 Prototyping-based.

    3.3.4 Cluster.

    3.3.6 Other _____.

3.4 - What techniques dominate your software process? (Circle one or more.)

    3.4.1 No systematic software technique.

    3.4.2 Structured analysis.

    3.4.3 Merise.

    3.4.4 JSD/JSP.

    3.4.5 Modular ("object-based", as in Ada-oriented approaches).

    3.4.6 Object-oriented.

    3.4.5 Other _____.

3.5 - What is the most common type of qualification among your software developers? (Circle one or, for a more precise answer, give percentages for each category. "Computing science education" includes formal training in programs whose possible official names include such variants as *computer science, computer engineering* and *information systems*.)

    3.5.1 No university-level education.

    3.5.2 University-level education but not in computing science.

    3.5.3 B.S. or equivalent (about 4 university years) in computing science.

    3.5.4 Masters' degree or equivalent (5 or 6 years) in computing science.

    3.5.5 PhD in computing science.

    3.5.6 Other _____.

compatibility: with an industry trend (1.1) or some of your partners (1.7). In this case one of your major concerns will be to make sure that your decisions are consistent with theirs. This may cause some headaches if the majority choices are not the best technical solutions (a regrettable but not infrequent situation).

If [B] is the dominant characteristic of your answers, then your main goal is **productivity**: turning out completed products faster (1.10) or more cheaply (1.12). The goal of benefiting from better tools (1.5) has been included in this category, even though the benefits may extend beyond productivity. But even if the [B] answers came from other questions the quality of the development environment should be a central criterion in your selection of a variant of object technology. You should also be looking for a language that is easy to learn, so as to avoid wasting time when you bring newcomers on board.

A [C] in first position, or close to it, indicates a preoccupation with quick **experimentation**, perhaps because in the past you have been plagued by systems that did not match user expectations, or developments whose flaws were not perceived until late in the projects. This is related to the previous case [B] but not identical, since [B] emphasizes fast development of *finished products*, not experiments. Here too the quality of the environment will play a prominent role; turnaround time (the time it takes to change part of an existing system, recompile it, and get it ready to run again) is critical. As to the language, ease of learning may be less important here than conciseness and power of expression, since you may perhaps prefer to put software experiments under the responsibility of a small, specialized team, which can initially take some time to get up to speed but will then be highly productive.

A prominent role for answers of types [D], [E] and [F] signals that your major concern, rather than productivity, is **quality**:

- With [D], you are preoccupied with **extendibility**: you want to be able to integrate changes quickly (1.6); this may be because you are largely concerned with the costs of maintenance (1.2).

- With [E], the accent is on **reliability**: avoiding introducing bugs in the first place (1.11) or, if bugs do appear, making it easier to correct them (1.3).

- With [F], finally, you have been won over by the promise of **reusability**: either as a consumer of existing components (1.4) or for the software of which you are a producer (1.9). (The discussion of reusability in chapter 6 will examine in detail the notions of reuse consumer and producer.)

In any one of these three cases, you should use a "pure" version of the object-oriented approach, not a hybrid one. Only a pure variant will enable you to get the expected quality benefits. In particular, case [E], reliability, suggests selecting a language with a built-in assertion mechanism and strong typing. Both for [E] and for [F] the availability of high-quality libraries of reusable components will be crucial.

Question 2 asks you to rate your group's proficiency with the method. As noted at the beginning of this chapter, experience with object-oriented analysis or design does not count if it did not lead to an object-oriented implementation. The best it can have given you is better readiness to accept some of the real stuff.

The borderline between "small" and "significant" has been set at 300 classes. This seems to be the approximate level up to which a group could still get away with an imperfect use of the object-oriented method, no systematic software engineering principles — and a fair amount of luck. Beyond that approximate limit luck will not save you. Scale and complexity require strict professional techniques, and if you are using an object-oriented language without applying the method you will be overwhelmed by inconsistency and inefficiency. The questions distinguish between projects using hybrid languages (2.5), for which it is difficult to ascertain that the group has applied the method thoroughly, and those using pure O-O languages (2.6 to 2.8), in which you do not really have a choice.

The answer to question 2 indicates in particular how much you may need training and consulting. If you are at level 2.3 or below, and probably 2.4 too, you should secure the proper outside help, especially if you are following the Bytex example and going at it on a large scale.

Question 3 will help you study your current software process. More extensive questionnaires are available; in particular, the SEI (Software Engineering Institute, an organization sponsored by the US Department of Defense and located in Pittsburgh) has widely publicized the "SEI maturity model", which defines a gradation of levels of software sophistication, from no rules to a highly formalized process. Question 3 is less ambitious but perhaps more directly helpful for evaluating how ready you are to embrace object technology.

A no answer to 3.1 and a yes answer to 3.2 indicate that many of your software choices are constrained by external partners. If, however, you are the one who pays, you should make sure that you are comfortable with the decisions taken, since you will have to live with the results — and possibly maintain them if you change supplier or the supplier fails you.

Inability to answer yes to 3.1 and 3.2 probably means that you have some delicate choices to make: if you both develop large parts of your software yourself and subcontract other large parts, you will need a solution that satisfies both your in-house process and your suppliers.

Question 3.3 asks about your process model. If your model is close but not identical to one of the well-known models appearing in the statement of the question, circle that one. If, as many large organizations, you use — or are supposed to use — some adaptation of the Waterfall (3.3.2), make sure to read chapter 3 in depth and to be prepared for a new approach to the overall organization of the software lifecycle: more seamless, less clearly divided into steps; more concurrent, less sequential; focused on producing actual executable results — code. If you use the spiral model (3.3.4), analyze what this brings you, and whether it would not be preferable to obtain final code earlier. If you think your model is based on prototyping, determine what this means in the classification of chapter 4, and how your current approach fits in with the rest of the object-oriented method.

3.4 addresses whether you use any method. It is a practical question, not a theoretical one; you should answer with what developers in your group actually do when they have to solve a software problem, not what they are supposed to do. "No systematic software technique" (3.4.1) is quite common, so do not be ashamed if that best describes your approach; you may just have been ahead of earlier methods, and waiting for object technology!

Structured analysis (3.4.2) is still the dominant technique in the MIS world and some other parts of the software community. Merise (3.4.3), also focused on information modeling, is not well known in the US but popular in some countries, in particular France where it originated. There have been extensive efforts to reconcile both Structured Analysis and Merise with object-oriented ideas, but the concepts remain remote. In particular, both of the older methods emphasize the *flow of information* and the *order* in which things happen, whereas the object-oriented approach views both of these aspects as not deserving early attention since they are subject to change. In my experience, software developers that have a deeply ingrained practice of these methods are in for a shock when moving to objects, and usually need retraining, with many practical case studies, before they really appropriate the new method. JSD/JSP (3.4.4), also known as the Jackson method, has been popular for years in England and a few other countries; although it emphasizes order too, it is probably, of the so-called traditional software methods, the one that best prepares for object orientation, in particular because of its emphasis on abstraction. Modular methods (3.4.5) are also a good preparation; often developed for use in connection with Ada, they incorporate some of the object-oriented ideas but not inheritance and all that follows from this notion.

> The statement of the question mentions (in quotes) the term *object-based* which is sometimes used to describe modular approaches, as distinct from *object-oriented*. This terminology is dubious, since the semantic nuance between "based" and "oriented", if any, is not striking. Adding to the confusion, many Ada-like approaches have been presented as "object-oriented".

The last question (3.5) addresses the educational background of the team that is targeted for introduction of object orientation. As noted, people with widely different kinds of prior education can become O-O experts; but they may need various levels and types of retraining. The discussion of needed skills (see "THE IDEAL O-O DEVELOPER PROFILE", page 87) shows what you should investigate: how much each person's education has emphasized *abstraction*, and how broad a spectrum of *computing science topics*, if any, it covered. More precisely:

- On the first point, mathematical and scientific education from a good high school and university, for example the standard scientific curriculum in French schools, is often the right preparation even if it was not specifically oriented towards computing. Good mathematicians, and good scientists from disciplines other than mathematics, will appreciate the object-oriented method for what it is — the application of the scientific mode of reasoning to software construction — and in general will pick it up quickly.

- On the second point, nothing matches a computing science education, covering a broad range of topics in programming languages, algorithms, data structures, operating systems, databases, some artificial intelligence techniques, and the other staple ingredients of a solid CS program.

For people who have had this kind of training, the difference between a four-year degree (3.5.3) and more advanced ones (3.5.4, 3.5.5) may be significant, as the latter typically require students, in a relatively short time, to master a number of new topics for which there may not exist single, well-known answers; this is excellent training for much of what goes on daily in the course of an advanced software project.

If members of the team lack a formal education, they may have made up for it through their hands-on experience; but do make sure you provide them with enough O-O training to get the concepts across.

BIBLIOGRAPHY

Roger F. Osmond: *Components of Success: Large Project Experience with Object Technology*, in *TOOLS 15*, (Technology of Object-Oriented Languages and Systems), Melbourne, Australia, ed. Christine Mingins, Prentice Hall, 1994.

> A reflection on the Bytex project discussed in the present chapter; written by the project's leader, also covers some of the later developments following from that project. Loaded with practical advice. A must read for any object-oriented project manager.

Bertrand Meyer: *Towards an Object-Oriented Curriculum*, in *Journal of Object-Oriented Programming*, vol. 6, no. 2, May 1993, pages 76-81.

> This article complements the discussion of industrial training in the present chapter by studying the use of O-O principles in an academic context. It emphasizes the applicability of object technology to many of the topics in the software curriculum, and particularly to the teaching of introductory programming. The method it advocates for teaching programming is an *inverted curriculum* where the course is based on an existing library of reusable components; instead of starting from trivial examples in a process where ontogeny repeats phylogeny, students are almost from day one given access to the power of a full-fledged library, which they first use as pure consumers to build significant applications. Little by little, through a process of *progressively opening the black boxes*, they learn how the components are made internally, how to adapt them to new uses, and how to build their own. An introductory textbook-cum-software based on these ideas (*Touch of Class*) is in preparation.

6

Nature and nurture: Making reuse succeed

One of the principal promises of the object-oriented method is a degree of reusability far superior to what the industry has known so far. But reuse will come only to those who understand the technology and know where to set their expectations.

Exploring practical issues of reusability will enable us to remove common misconceptions, and to study the details of *generalization*, the new activity introduced in the study of the lifecycle, which is so characteristic of a proper application of the method.

One general observation before we immerse ourselves in the delights and pitfalls of reusable software construction: if reusability is not (or is not yet) your thing, this does not necessarily mean that something is wrong with you! Important as reusability is among the potential benefits of the O-O method, it is not the only one, and there are perfectly legitimate reasons besides it for going to objects — building software faster (the productivity benefit), making it more reliable and easier to change (the quality benefits). But you should still read this chapter: it will show how you can benefit from *other people*'s reuse efforts, and what to expect when and if you decide to make reusability a central part of your own plans.

THE TWO VIEWS OF REUSE

The first observation, when assessing how the object-oriented method can help achieve more reusability, is to understand what we are after. There are two aspects to reuse, and they should not be confused.

The **consumer's view** of reuse applies when an organization decides to base its software development on existing reusable components. This will be the case, for example, if you acquire a good object-oriented environment that comes fully equipped with quality libraries covering such areas as basic data structures, fundamental algorithms and graphics.

The **producer's view** of reuse applies to an organization that is devoting reusability concerns to the software that it develops, making this software or some of its components general enough to be reusable by other projects.

The normal way to proceed, for a company that is moving to object orientation, is to start as a consumer of reuse: acquire, study and apply a good reusable library. After a while, the company will be ready to produce its own reusable software — if that is part of its aims.

WHY REUSABILITY?

That increasing software reusability is a worthy goal has by now become conventional wisdom in the software world.

> It was not always so. Around 1982, a paper of mine submitted to an IEEE software conference came back with the referee's dismissive comment that "reusability" was not a proper English word. Things have changed: one can surmise that nowadays a submission to an IEEE software conference might be rejected on the grounds that it does *not* use this word.

But that an idea is now well received to the point of having almost become a buzzword does not mean that we should accept it without question. In particular, if you are pushing object technology in your company it is important to use the right arguments.

Making software reusable holds a number of promises:

ARGUMENTS FOR REUSABILITY

1 • Enhancing productivity (C).

2 • Facilitating maintenance (C)

3 • Improving reliability (C).

4 • Improving efficiency (C).

5 • Improving interoperability (C/P).

6 • Capitalizing on the software investment (P).

(C): Follows from reuse as consumer.
(P): Follows from reuse as producer.

As indicated, some of these benefits can be derived from a pure consumer's view of reuse, others from becoming a reuse producer.

The most frequently considered argument is number 1 (enhancing productivity): by reusing software, you have less software to develop, and you can bring your products to market faster.

Not to be overlooked is point 2 (facilitating maintenance): if others are responsible for the product, they are also responsible for corrections and adaptations. In an industry which is often devoting 50% to 80% of its resources to maintenance, this is a precious benefit; reuse can enable you to devote your efforts to new applications, not to the backlog of maintaining existing applications. There is of course another, less enticing side: since you are not fully in control of the software, you depend on someone else to update it when needed. But anyone who knows the reality of software development — the more successful software you produce, the more future work you are creating for yourself — will readily appreciate the advantages of offloading responsibility for the least specific parts of the development.

Point 3 (improving reliability) is in my experience the most important benefit of reuse. By relying on reusable software from a reputable source, you gain the expectation that it will have far fewer bugs than software that has just been developed for the occasion. Not necessarily because its authors are smarter; not even just because, being in the business of producing the components (rather than writing software elements that are auxiliary to some other application) they must have been careful; but also because the components, by their very nature, will have been exercised by many others before you. In the practice of ISE, this is probably the major argument for using libraries: any developer in our company can put together a linked list class rather quickly, but that is not what we do when we need such a data structure; we rely instead on the corresponding classes from the EiffelBase library, known to have been satisfactorily used by many people. Roger Osmond of Bytex (see "A SUCCESS STORY", page 85) also cited the availability of these libraries as a key success factor.

Point 4 (improving efficiency) follows from the same general observation. Interestingly, when most people think of the relationship between reusability and efficiency, they first see the reverse effect: reusability, meaning emphasis on generality, may render impossible certain optimizations that depend on precise knowledge of application-specific details. But this is a microscopic view of efficiency. In practice, no one optimizes every single detail of a 500,000 line program. Much more likely is the risk of using non-optimal solutions for those numerous aspects of the program that are not application-specific. For example if you are writing a large switching system your emphasis will be in optimizing the telecommunications aspects; this is where your team's expertise lies. You may not devote as much attention to auxiliary aspects such as data structures. By relying on reusable solutions for these non-application-specific aspects you benefit from the expertise of people — the library authors — for whom these components *are* the application.

Point 5 (improving interoperability) is due to a feature of good reusable software: it enforces consistency and compatibility. The book *Reusable Software...* (see the bibliography at the end of this chapter) shows how the design of a good library requires a stringent approach to the consistency of design styles, interface specifications and naming conventions. Even if you are just a consumer of reuse, this will have an excellent effect, as the design principles of the library filter over, through a process of osmosis and imitation, to your own software. This promoted a form of **egoless programming**: software developed by different people will tend to follow the same general design and interface conventions, facilitating interoperability and future evolution.

> "Egoless programming" was a slogan of the software management literature of the seventies and early eighties, and has somewhat passed out of fashion. Taken as an invitation to bridle programmer creativity, it is a bad idea: programming is a challenging intellectual activity, not a repetitive production process amenable to Taylor-like standardization. A good manager will want to encourage creativity, not censor it. But egoless programming remains desirable if we take it to mean that creativity, far from being suppressed, should be channeled into the areas where it can bring real benefits— invention of smart technical solutions at all levels, from specification to implementation — whereas anything that affects the communication between modules and between developers should be standardized, not left to individual whims.

Finally point 6 (capitalizing on your software investment) is the intended benefit of reuse in the producer's sense: making software reusable turns a virtual asset, the knowledge and experience of your best developers, into a tangible investment — components.

Of these possible benefits, some will be more important to your organization than others. It is important to know what you are after. In particular, the consumer benefits of reuse may be sufficient, at least initially, for many companies.

STACKS OR CUSTOMERS?

> *They say Stacks are trivial. They say Stacks are too abstract. They want to know when we'll do something real, like encapsulate an airplane or a database. Answer: They will never get there if they can't handle a Stack first.*
>
> James McKim, JOOP, July-August 1994 (see the bibliography).

The strategy of starting as a reuse consumer and progressing to reuse producer seems so obvious that one should not have to justify it. Yet in discussions with many managers from industry I have found that this simple idea is far from being universally accepted. In particular, many people seem to think that by switching to object-oriented development they can start producing reusable software right away. This is nonsense.

Building reusable components is difficult. Reusable object-oriented software must *first* be object-oriented software of the highest possible quality, and *additionally* be reusable. This is not stuff for the newcomer; the art of producing reusable components is learned by imitation and hard work.

That was the bad news. The good news is that if you set your expectations right and begin in earnest as a consumer, you can quickly gain great benefits from reuse; and at some later point you will be ready to move from student to master — from consumer to producer.

Misplaced and exaggerated expectations often take the form of a request for **business objects**. Careless O-O literature seems to have succeeded in convincing a large number of software managers that they can quickly and painlessly produce reusable components that directly address the specifics of their business — classes describing their company's notion of customer, inventory item, automobile part, soft drink bottle, or whatever the major concepts are in its line of business. These are business *classes*, of course, not business objects; but let us not quibble since this is the least part of the misunderstanding.

Curiously, every discussion of this kind that I have had with managers seems sooner or later to come down to stacks versus customers. Stop talking to me about your Stack class, the argument will go; what I want is the Customer "object". Stacks and Customers are taken here as representatives of two different categories of potential components:

- Stacks are the usual paradigm for "computing-sciency" stuff, the basic data structures and algorithms — lists, queues, table, sorting and the like, what we may call *Knuthware* in honor of the most famous scholar in this field. More generally, this category should also include general-purpose components covering such needs as graphics, user interfaces (windows, widgets, menus, ...), database access, formal language analysis (lexing, parsing), and others that extend across application areas.

- Customers are taken as the typical example of abstraction that directly covers a business need.

It would be nice to be able to say: "Yes, you can immediately start writing your reusable *CUSTOMER* class, and it will provide you with reuse beyond your wildest dreams". Unfortunately, this is not true; nor should this cause any despair, or any claim that "O-O is not delivering on the reuse promise!". We need a more cool-headed appraisal.

LEARNING BEFORE JUMPING

The first observation that helps resolve the "Stacks or Customers?" debate has already been made: one has to start somewhere, and be an apprentice before becoming a expert. You will not be able to produce reusable components of your own before you have understood a significant number of existing components by using and studying them. The components on which you will rely for this process will likely be general-purpose ones (more similar to *STACK* than to *CUSTOMER*), if only because they are the most readily available.

Another reason for focusing on general-purpose components first is that they have benefited from a better established theory. Knuthware has been studied by computer scientists for more than three decades. Stacks, for example, are well-known beasts, with plenty of theory to explain their eating and digesting habits. Business-related animals such as customers are much less well understood. It is natural, to start with the notions that have clear and convincing descriptions.

The situation for business classes may actually be worse: perhaps there does not exist a description of the *CUSTOMER* abstraction that, in your current understanding of your business, will be satisfactory to everyone. The marketing department, the accounting department, the customer service department and the engineering department may all have their views of what a customer is, and they may not be compatible.

This observation sets the limits of what you can expect from business classes when you do get ready to consider them: it is useless to try writing reusable components unless the underlying abstractions are properly understood. This does not mean restricting yourself to components that are as well defined mathematically as stacks; but there must be enough accepted knowledge to enable defining and implementing a proper set of abstractions.

> Scientists and engineers know this rule well: if you are working in any domain and wish to carry out actions that will affect the situation in that domain — for example by building engineering devices if the domain is physics, or by devising investment strategies if your domain is economics — you need a rational *model* (or *theory*) of that domain. For stacks and the like, the models exist, and may be found in the computing science literature; for a notion such as customer, models may be possible, but they are not as readily available. Until you have found such a model, it is as futile to try to build a reusable *CUSTOMER* class as it would be for an engineer to try to build a flying machine without a good model of fluid dynamics.

Even if you initially find few business examples that fit these requirements, this is not a reason to give up on reuse. General-purpose components can already improve the software development process and products by a considerable factor.

Here then is the first answer to the hurried manager's imperious "Keep your stacks, give me my customers!" request: look at the reality of software development in your company; this will probably reveal that developers spend most of their time dealing not with the *CUSTOMER* abstraction but indeed with stacks, queues, lists, hash tables, binary trees, arrays, as well as graphical objects, database access and operating system interfaces.

When told this, our manager might retort "But that's precisely what's wrong! We don't have enough of a business focus around here!". Perhaps true, but not an argument for dismissing the utility of general-purpose components. In fact, this is an argument for just the reverse. The reason why programmers spend their time on programming problems — which the manager considers low-level stuff — rather than business-related software issues may well be that they have to reinvent and debug the low-level part again and again. By relying on reusable components for the aspects that are common to your application and to thousands of others, you can free the resources and intelligence of your team to work on the parts that really distinguish your business from others.

So the much maligned general-purpose components — classes *STACK*, *WINDOW* and the like — can be fundamental in enabling the developers to concentrate on the parts of their software that directly address the company's business. If for those business-related elements you are not immediately able to obtain or produce reusable components — business classes — this does not mean that O-O and reuse have failed you. With a little more time and experience, you may be able to isolate business abstractions; and in the meantime, the presence of good general-purpose reusable components might transform your software development process in ways that you would not even dream of at first, and enable you to concentrate on the issues of real interest to you and your organization.

This discussion can be summed up by a simple piece of advice:

PRAGMATISM IN REUSE PRINCIPLE

Scorn Not The Humble Stack.

ORGANIZING FOR REUSABILITY

Assume now that you have done your apprenticeship as a reuse consumer and you are ready for the real thing — building your own base of reusable components so as to gain the full benefits of the object-oriented approach.

This can be a smooth and progressive process; but it is important to organize it appropriately and to avoid a number of common mistakes and misconceptions. Two ingredients are necessary, neither of which needs to be as grandiose as the names may initially suggest:

• A **reusability policy**.

• A **reusability manager**.

The reusability policy defines the scope and goals of the company's reusability efforts. It should be described in a document, the *reusability plan*. The most important contribution of the reusability plan is to send a message from management that reuse is considered important; that beyond the immediate project goals — delivering quality results on time and within budget — the company also values every contribution that enriches its global software assets. Concretely, the reusability plan will specify the procedures to be applied for accepting candidate reusable components, and the people in charge of applying these procedures.

The reusability manager is the person in charge of advancing the cause of reusability in the organization, and implementing the reusability policy. Initially this does not have to be a full-time job, but may be an extra responsibility added to someone's existing duties.

For a small organization, or one that is only starting a small-scale reusability effort, having one person (the reusability manager) in charge of the policy will be enough. To move on to the next level, you will need a **reusability group**, reporting to the reusability manager. Later on in this chapter we will see why its members should not be called "librarians", and why their work is actually comparable to that of software developers working on specific projects.

THE TWO MYTHS OF SOFTWARE REUSABILITY

Among the main obstacles to the improvement of reusability in the software industry are two misconceptions that are almost universally held by managers in the field:

1 • The impression that logistics aspects, such as databases of reusable components, query facilities, component retrieval systems and network access mechanisms are the most difficult issues in widening the impact of reuse, or among the most difficult. We will be so flooded with components, the idea goes, that without elaborate mechanisms we will spend as much effort finding our way through them as we would developing our own software using non-reusable solutions.

2 • The perception that another major problem is the programmers' typical reluctance to reuse someone else's creations — the famous "Not Invented Here" (NIH) syndrome.

It is impossible to make your organization progress towards reuse if you believe either of these myths. Let us clear them.

View 1 is absurd. Even if it were true that finding components is hard, this would still leave all but the first of the benefits studied above — reliability, interoperability and so on. But that is not even the problem. What can hamper the progress of reuse is the difficulty of producing reusable components, not the difficulty of organizing them!

Thinking of reuse and focusing on these organizational problems is about the same as deciding to become a multimillionaire and worrying about how hard it will be to find people to look after the castle in the Loire valley and the yacht on the Riviera. Sure, good domestics are hard to come by these days; but comparatively that is the easy part of the problem; should we not think first about how we will find the money to buy the things in the first place?

View 1 can only be held by people who have no experience of building reusable software. Anyone who has produced successful components knows the intellectual challenges that this goal poses. Once you have the components, you must organize them properly, of course, and make them easily retrievable by whoever may be interested. But that is the easy part. It is a database problem; the customer database of the average company contains more information, and more information links, than will ever be present in the company's repertory of reusable components over the next twenty years.

One of the distinctive traits of a good engineer and of a good manager is an ability to separate the difficult problems from the less difficult ones, and to devote the primary efforts to the first category. In software reuse, the challenge is building the components. The rest needs to be done carefully, of course, like everything else — like hiring a keeper for your palace and a skipper for your yacht, once these properties are yours — but will be nowhere near as hard.

Now for view 2, the myth of the NIH syndrome. It is just as wrong as view 1. The reason is easy to understand: most programmers are human beings; and very few human beings like to work hard to reach a goal if they can reach that goal by working less.

Software developers, not surprisingly, react in the same way. Give them good reusable components, and they will swallow them faster than you can say "Not Invented Here", then ask for more. The evidence is there in the non-object-oriented world: the hundreds of Unix, DOS and Windows utilities that countless people use for their daily work — tools with strange names such as sed, awk, yacc, lex, perl and many more. Few people nowadays, for example, write a parser (syntactic analyzer) from scratch in ordinary circumstances; this task, which was once considered a major software development, is now routinely addressed by reusable components. In the past few years, the movement has amplified: dozens of nifty tools have appeared, which you can download from the network and try for your own development. The good ones spread like wildfire.

So far this phenomenon has mostly affected coarse-grain components such as operating system utilities, and has not yet reached with the same intensity the level of software components to be integrated in programs, the reason being the obvious technical one: quality reusable components require the full extent of object technology, and, as emphasized in this chapter, require hard work. But the precedent is clear. No competent developer will develop new software if a good reusable solution is available instead.

> There is the occasional exception, of course — the programmer who insists on redoing everything. A name exists for such people: bad programmers. They are probably the same who do not comment their programs and use arcane designs that no one else can comprehend or maintain. Such programmers, unless retrained, have no place in today's software industry.

Why then this perception of the NIH syndrome? Managers did not completely make it up. But the reality that it reflects is quite different from the appearances. What you do see in practice is developers who are leery of reusable components *because they have been burned before*. Anything can have gone wrong: a component that did not perform as advertised, was buggy, poorly documented or too slow, relied on assumptions which did not transpose to the reuser's environment, was not flexible enough, only came with object code and bad customer support... It does not take too many such experiences to become a fervent nonbeliever in reuse. But that is not the fault of the component consumer; it is the fault of the components.

CHASING THE RIGHT HORSE

Debunking the two myths of reusability leads to an observation that will guide the rest of this discussion:

> **REUSE PRIORITIES PRINCIPLE**
>
> The difficult issues of reuse are almost entirely producer issues, not consumer issues.

The most common error of managers who become interested in reuse is to think that it is a consumer issue: that the problem is to convince developers to use reusable components. With such an approach the reusability policy will mean going out and holding reuse preaching sessions where developers are exhorted to repent their sins and turn their cheeks to other people's software.

Such an approach is misplaced. Good developers do not need to be told to reuse; they need to be given good components.

It never hurts, of course, to remind people once in a while of the importance of reuse; but rather than a reusability policy this is simply part of the normal process of continuous education, similar to reminding developers to use object technology, apply the company's or projects's methodological rules, comment their software properly, leave adequate documentation, and more generally follow good software engineering practices, of which reuse is but an element.

For an example of a company that has not understood these principles, see "EXERCISE: WHAT ARE THESE PEOPLE DOING WRONG?", page 129

The problem is to foster the production of quality reusable components. This is not the *only* problem of reuse, but it is the only difficult one. Solve it, and everything else will follow. The responsibilities are clear:

REUSABILITY POLICY PRINCIPLE

The goal of a reusability policy is to satisfy the customers (the potential reusers of components) by prevailing on the producers (the writers of components) to do the best possible job.

If you are in charge of promoting reuse within your organization, spending your time chasing the potential consumers to convince them to reuse more is a betrayal of your mission. Developers have jobs to do — software to develop. They do it in the best of their abilities. If they choose a bad solution, their job will not get done and *they* will be in trouble.

It is not the programmers' responsibility to listen to your admonitions about reusability. It is *your* responsibility to provide them with reusable components so good that they will not want to program without them.

One case, seen later in this chapter, justifies directing reusability awareness efforts towards consumers. It arises when the reusability policy has reached a first level of success and teams that have been using components may be tempted to extend or adapt them in various ways, at the risk of diverging from the common version. See "THE DISCIPLINE OF REUSABILITY", page 128.

THE LIBRARY

Because the key to success in reuse is in the producers' hands, the reusability policy must carefully define what is acceptable as a reusable component.

A central component of the reusability policy, then, is the specification of a corporate *library* that will contain approved reusable components, and of the criteria that govern approval of candidate components. The responsibility for defining and applying these criteria rests with the reusability manager.

How strict should the criteria be? Companies that are starting on the path to reuse often tend to take a lenient attitude, on the grounds that it is hard enough to get developers to volunteer candidate components, so that the few who do should be encouraged. This attitude goes against the Reusability Policy Principle: it kowtows to the producers, and as a result endangers the future of reuse in the company by leading to components of insufficient quality which, as noted, will put off the potential consumers and make them distrustful of *any* reusable solutions. You should instead apply the following rule:

> ### LIBRARY ENTRY PRINCIPLE
>
> No software element should be accepted into the library unless it meets a set of quality criteria, defined precisely by the organization as part of its reusability policy.

The criteria must be reasonable but demanding: no company should compromise on the quality requirements for reusable components. Everything counts: substance, of course (design decisions, inheritance hierarchies, information hiding) but also form (consistency, naming, interface style).

Chapter 3 of the book *Reusable Software...* (see the bibliography at the end of this chapter) contains a detailed list of reusability rules which can yield your initial set of criteria.

By trying not to put off the consumers, will a strict acceptance policy risk offending the producers and so put reuse in jeopardy anyway? Normally no. The key is in how you handle the rejection. "Go home, you fool!" will not gain you any friends. Instead, you should return to the submitter an evaluation report stating precisely the criteria that caused rejection, and sketching what should be done to make the components acceptable for inclusion.

Such a constructive answer will encourage submitters to revise and resubmit the components. It may in fact come to be considered normal that the first version be rejected. The process of producing good reusable components is always iterative anyway — especially if you apply the *generalization* approach, described later in this chapter, which promotes producing components by extracting some of the best elements of specific (non-reusable) projects and improving them. An earlier chapter noted that this approach to reusability is the aspect of O-O development that most appropriately evokes traditional, non-software notions of prototyping ("PROTOTYPING FOR REUSABILITY?", page 70).

Setting the stakes high is your only way to guarantee that the library will not disappoint its intended users. It may mean that the library will initially and for some time have few components; but that is to be accepted: better a small library than a poor-quality one. In any case, the policy of starting out as a reuse consumer, described at the beginning of this chapter, means that you should initially build up the library from components acquired outside, so it may already be sizable before you accept your first in-house development into it.

Serious acceptance criteria are also a good way to catch the attention of software developers. Having one's components accepted into the library should be considered an honor — a success similar to what happens in other engineering fields when a company obtains a patent on an invention made by one of its engineers.

The existence of precise library inclusion criteria also helps clarify a question that is sometimes raised in connection with reuse: material rewards. Some discussions in the literature suggest offering bonuses to developers who produce reusable components. A few companies have indeed tried this approach. Is this a good or a bad idea? There is no absolute answer; what you will decide depends on your management culture and on how it rewards individual initiative. But on one point the rule seems clear: if you do have such rewards in place, you should bestow them on the basis of acceptance into the library. If the criteria are explicit and demanding, the first test of reusability success is to meet them.

The final test, as noted, is actual reuse. For that reason, some companies may prefer incentives based not just on initial library acceptance but also on the amount of reuse by other projects.

THE REPOSITORY

A natural objection to the insistence on tight library inclusion criteria is that sometimes a company may need to ensure the preservation of some software expertise even if the corresponding components are not of optimal quality. This may happen for various reasons:

- The company may fear losing some of its assets. The concern for preserving software investment has grown in the past few years as the authors of legacy applications developed in the sixties and seventies get closer to retirement. (In the computer field it once seemed that everyone around you was young. Well, some of these people are not so young any more; in fact computerfolk age and retire like everyone else.) This understandably makes companies nervous, and it may be tempting to accept a component into the library simply to avoid the loss of the corresponding expertise.

- In other cases, someone may volunteer a component which is not quite up to the library's standard, but for which no resources are available to perform the work needed to bring it there. You may feel then that an imperfect component is better than no component.

- Yet another typical situation arises from redundant components. The preceding analysis of the requirements for a library lead us to consider redundancies as something to be frowned upon. If consumer convenience is what guides our policy, the presence of two components that address the same need is neither good nor neutral, but actually bad: instead of selecting one of the alternatives we have unloaded the choice on the library users. Yet in some cases you might want to keep alternate components anyway — not knowing which one of the alternatives is better, or whether they might actually cover subtly different needs.

All these cases seem to provide legitimate reasons for relaxing the rules for library inclusion. But you must not take such a risk. The library is the officially approved repertoire of quality components; you cannot afford to endanger its reputation. Caving in to the producers means alienating your real constituency — the consumers.

The solution, when the need for lesser-grade components becomes too pressing, is to introduce a second collection of components, separate from the library. Let us call it the *repository*. Criteria for inclusion into the repository are much more lax; you may accept anything that looks reasonable. The repository will be the natural place for components that may duplicate the functionality of some others or that have only reached at a less-than-ideal quality level, but that you still want to make available, sometimes only for diplomatic reasons. What is essential here is to avoid deceptive advertizing: whereas the library is the collection of officially supported components, the documentation for the repository should clearly state that its components are "Use at Your Own Risk". This also makes it possible to use the repository as a purgatory for any future library components that you want to make available before they have reached perfection.

Some companies have implemented more complex schemes. I have discussed the issue with the reusability managers of a large aerospace company that has an active reusability policy. Concerned about the possible loss of valuable contributions (the legacy problem), that company has set up an extensive matrix to characterize each component's status vis-à-vis a number of reusability criteria. A simpler approach seems preferable; developers will be content with a binary classification: officially approved (the library) versus non-guaranteed (the repository).

THE TWO PATHS TO PRODUCING REUSABLE SOFTWARE

On the key notions of reusability policy and library, a number of issues remain to be addressed: how should you manage the library? How will it evolve over time? Who is going to pay for all this?

Before we can answer these questions, however, we need to understand the process of producing components. Without a mechanism that will produce a continuous stream of new components, there is neither a library nor a reusability policy. As noted, the library should be initialized with quality components acquired from the outside, which will start the company on the path to reuse and provide models to follow. But after that how do we go about producing our own components?

Two approaches are possible:

- The **direct approach**: you may decide from the start that you need a reusable component addressing a certain need, and build it accordingly. This process happens in particular in companies that are officially in the business of producing components, especially vendors of O-O tools and libraries (such as ISE), and in the still rare companies which have established a comprehensive library development effort for their own internal software needs. This may also be called the *a priori* approach.

- The **indirect approach**: in the common situation where a program element has been produced to meet some immediate requirement rather than for posterity, all is not necessarily lost for reusability. If similar needs are likely to occur again, the module's quality shows good promise, and the company's software development process encourages reusability, then the incentives will be there to spend more time making the module reusable. Generalization, the new step of the lifecycle introduced in chapter 3 (see the cluster lifecycle diagram on page 53), is this *a posteriori* process of producing software components from program elements.

The debate between these two approaches has also been called the "nature versus nurture" issue (hence the title to this chapter): is reusability an innate trait, or is it acquired? Are great components born or made?

To avoid any confusion in the discussion, here again is the equivalent terminology used on each side:

APPROACHES TO REUSE: TERMINOLOGY	
(Approach 1)	*(Approach 2)*
A priori	A posteriori
Direct	Indirect
Nature	Nurture

If you are expecting the debate to end up in a reconciliation of the adversaries, you have guessed right; but that predictable outcome is not the most important point of the discussion which follows. What matters is to understand what each approach has to bring, and how you can combine them.

ARGUMENTS FOR NATURE AND FOR NURTURE

The principal argument for the a priori approach can be summed up simply:

> ### A PRIORI PRINCIPLE
>
> Reusability cannot be added as an afterthought.

Unless you have integrated the concern for reuse early in your design process you have little chance of being able to turn your program elements into software components later on. Reusability is not an add-on; it is a culture. The culture of reusability implies a constant obsession for generality and consistency, and invites software designers, in addition to all the questions that they have to address, to ask themselves for each new design decision the two key questions of reusability:

- How do I make this design decision without insulting the past — that is to say, so that the decision is not only satisfactory for the goal that I am pursuing now but also compatible with the myriad decisions that have been made (by myself but also by many others) before?

- How do I make this design decision so that I will not regret it later — that is to say, so as to make it possible in the future (for myself but also for many others) to make *new* design decisions that will be compatible with what I am deciding today?

This is a demanding discipline. Trying to follow it does not guarantee a 100% success rate, but unless you try you will not go very far on the path to reusable software construction.

To this the a posteriori school might reply with another one-liner:

> ### A POSTERIORI PRINCIPLE
>
> No software is reusable until it has been reused.

This carries the implication that no software will be reusable the first time around. The observation is that it is extremely difficult to avoid leaving in your software implicit assumptions about the environment — assumptions which will be true when you design and try out the software, but may not hold any more in the environment of potential reusers working in a different company, a different country, or simply under different intellectual models of software development.

We may distinguish four levels of reusability for a software module (level 0 achieves usability but not yet reusability):

LEVELS OF MODULE REUSABILITY

0 • Used successfully in one system.

1 • Used in several systems produced by the module's author.

2 • Used in systems produced by the author's colleagues.

3 • Used in systems produced by other people, all of whom the author knows about.

4 • Used in systems produced by people of whom the author has never heard.

Each progression to a new level on this list brings a new set of requirements since it may reveal hidden assumptions on the environment. Moving to level 1 means removing dependencies on the original application. At level 2, the people reusing your module are working in the same company, or at least are intellectually close to you — but they are not you, so some of your assumptions may turn out not to be valid any more.

When you move to level 3, you start delivering your purportedly reusable software to people outside of your circle; that may again cause some surprises. At level 3, however, you still know individually who your customers are.

At level 4, this is not true any more: people know about your software even though you do not know about them.

> The clearest sign is when you get a user report — usually angry — from someone in a faraway place, about whom you know nothing, complaining about something that does not work as the user would like it to. Then you know you have succeeded.

The A Posteriori Principle simply asserts that all the a priori precautions in the world will not guarantee that you can move from each level to the next. Until you have reused the module in a new development, you have no proof that you can reuse it; until one of your colleagues has applied it successfully, you have no proof that anyone else can reuse it; until someone in a completely different environment has been able to rely on it, you have no proof that it is not tied to a specific way of working; and only when it gets used by some total stranger will you have full evidence of its reusability.

The implicit lesson of the A Posteriori Principle is of course more pessimistic — the idea that each such progression from a level of reuse to the next will uncover problems and require modifications. As you get reports from the field, reflecting the experiences of people further and further away from you, trying to apply your component to goals further and further away from yours, you may have to rework it repeatedly until it is truly general.

THE MÉTHODE CHAMPENOISE

The indirect approach (nurture) relies on the A Posteriori Principle to produce reusable software components not out the blue, but by a process of generalizing program elements drawn from successful applications.

Inferior as it may theoretically seem, the indirect approach deserves careful attention; for a company that wishes to increase reuse but is not ready to overhaul all its software development practices, it provides a smoother transition to the role of reuse producer. This approach would perhaps better be called the *méthode champenoise*: instead of impatiently trying to get all the bubbles in at once, we start from a young and immature (but strong and attractive) blend, and nurture it lovingly until it tastes ripe enough for release.

This approach has a clear advantage over the direct one: because it yields reusable components only after a detour through program elements, it avoids the risk of producing modules that look good to the library designer but do not solve anyone's real problems, or place unrealistic requirements on the reusers (the future consumers). This is reflected in two requirements that complement the A Posteriori Principle:

USEFULNESS PRINCIPLE

No software is reusable unless it is useful.

USABILITY PRINCIPLE

No software is reusable unless it is usable.

The indirect approach can only work, however, in special conditions. Carbonate bland white wine and add a fancy label, the result will still be sweet bubbly. In the same way, any amount of effort applied to ordinary modules is unlikely to yield software components of a lasting value. As noted above, the production of reusable software requires strict design principles and a constant concern for consistency. So the indirect approach can only be successful if it is applied by a group which has acquired an in-depth experience as a reuse consumer; a group that is aware of the difficulties of reuse, has been extensively using a set of high-quality libraries, understands the design principles behind these libraries, and is prepared to design its own software in a manner compatible with these principles even for modules which at least provisionally will just be program elements. This will later enable the reusability manager to pick the most interesting of these elements and generalize them into software components, without having to pay the price of constant redesign.

Things do not proceed otherwise when, at the end of the season, the chief œnologist takes a walk around the cool high-vaulted limestone cellars to sample the nectar from the husky oak barrels, separating the year's ordinary output, soon to be sold as table wine, from what after much further toil will ultimately become the *grands crus millésimés*, pride and profit of the estate.

Applied in an organization that thinks about reuse from the start, the indirect approach has its role along with the direct one. Our experience at ISE confirms the usefulness of combining the two methods. Much of our work is to develop libraries of reusable components, naturally following the direct approach (although it never hurts to draw inspiration from existing program elements addressing similar needs). For developments of a more traditional nature, those which are initially meant to solve specific problems rather than to yield reusable components, we have found it fruitful to follow the preceding advice, fostering what an earlier section of this chapter called the *culture of reusability*; we constantly keep in mind the concern for potential reuse by adhering to a consistent set of design principles, based on the observation and imitation of our libraries. We have also found that a such a policy does not interfere with the usual constraints and pressures of specific software development; if anything, it tends to help. Most importantly, it provides a second source of reusable components, to be derived later through generalization.

The practice of generalization, once an organization has understood the importance of this task, tends to influence the development of all software, including software meant from the start to be reusable. You learn not to release components too quickly, because there is really no way to make sure that a class is reusable until it has been reused; and the first few attempts at reuse may uncover limitations or deficiencies of the class for its intended role as component of a widely distributed library.

So you should not rush. Tokyo and New York may be clamoring for the first batch of the year's Beaujolais Nouveau, but the proud vintner knows not to release the production before it has had the time to age properly in the barrel or the bottle.

MERGING THE TWO APPROACHES

With the policy just described, the opposition between the direct and indirect approaches fades away. The difference between a program element and a software component becomes a question of degree, not of nature. Every module is designed under the assumption that it will eventually become part of a reusable library; but no module is immediately included in the library. In this meritocracy of modules, no one is born reusable; everyone must graduate into reusability. Some, of course, graduate faster than others.

This process of continuous improvement of class libraries and their structure, this search for order where perfection is never reached but evidence of progress is unmistakable, accounts for some of the most rewarding aspects of object-oriented software development. Like a good cellar, a good library becomes ever better with age through improvements both to each individual component and to the overall selection and organization of components.

As often in science, the general direction (defeating the second law of thermodynamics) is from the complex to the simple, from chaos to order. The first version of a library often includes useless complications, and it is only after further reflection that one discovers the underlying simplicity — like a mathematician who goes through a messy, intuitive, indirect and sweaty process to produce a theory or a proof which, once polished and refined, will look orderly, formal, immediate and effortless.

This process of refining a library is intellectually satisfying, as you make the result of your software efforts ever more powerful and elegant; but it is also economically sound,

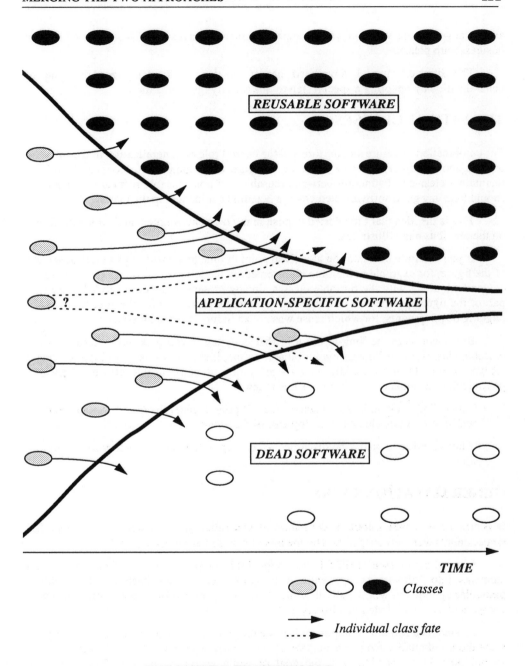

REUSABLE SOFTWARE

APPLICATION-SPECIFIC SOFTWARE

DEAD SOFTWARE

TIME

Classes

Individual class fate

THE FUTURE OF THE WORLD
(*BE REUSED OR DIE*)

See "THE FATE OF CLASSES", page 122

as you augment the value of your company's software investment — a case of mixing business with pleasure.

The lifecycle model developed earlier in this book recognizes the role of generalization by devoting a special step to this activity: generalization.

THE FATE OF CLASSES

The combination of nature and nurture and the central role of generalization in the software process model affect the very spirit of software development. No longer should we maintain a clear-cut distinction between reusable and non-reusable software. Instead, we should treat any good software element as a potential component in the making.

This is the idea that I have tried to push in my own environment and which the figure on the previous page illustrates.

If you examine the situation at a given point in time by considering a vertical section of the figure, for example at the time represented by the leftmost vertical axis, you will of course find, along with the reusable classes already present in the company's library (top part of the figure), some non-reusable classes (middle part) built for the specific needs of ongoing developments, for which reuse was not an immediate design goal.

But if you take the long-term view, that is to say if you pick any one of the non-reusable classes and follow its evolution along time, it should not be permitted to remain forever in the shrinking middle area — the limbo of non-reusable classes. Only two possible fates await such a class in this ideal view:

- If it is good enough, it will at some time fall prey to generalization fever and join the world of reusable classes in the top area of the figure.

- If not, it will eventually be discarded — end up in the class cemetery in the bottom area.

GENERALIZATION TASKS

It is now time to take a look at the nature of generalization, this step of the Clusterfall whose details were left unspecified by the model's presentation in chapter 3.

Generalization (see "THE STEPS", page 54) is the process of transforming program elements into software components. A program element has been developed for a particular system and will usually be dependent on the context of that system. A software component can be included in a library and reused by many different systems.

Producing a software component is more difficult than producing a program element, since the usual quality requirements (the element must be correct, it must be efficient and so on) must be reconciled with the goal of being useful to many different software developers in many different contexts. Certain deficiencies which may be tolerable in a program element, because the developers completely control the context of its usage, will not pass muster for a software component.

What activities are involved in the generalization step?

Some follow directly from the reusability concern and would be useful with any reuse-seeking method, object-oriented or not:

- Improving the documentation to make the component usable by consumers that do not necessarily know the implicit assumptions that guided its original development.

- Improving the robustness of the components, since for library usage, where the client applications can be of many different kinds, you have less control over possible abnormal cases.

- Improving their efficiency.

More specific to this discussion is a set of other generalization activities applicable only in the object-oriented context and intended to improve the module interconnection structure — especially the inheritance graph, which reflects how the designers understand the structure of the application domain and are able to classify their knowledge of it.

These activities belong to two related categories: **abstracting** and **factoring**.

Abstracting is the late recognition of higher-level concepts. The developers may have written a class B which covers a useful notion. But they did not recognize that it was actually a special case of a more general notion A, so that it should have used an inheritance hierarchy of the form

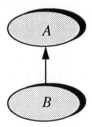

In a perfect world the developers would first have identified the higher-level abstraction, A, then its variant B. But the world is not perfect. With a generalization process in place, you may recognize *ex post facto* the need for A. It is not as good as having identified it earlier, but better than not identifying it at all.

Factoring is the case in which you detect that two classes E and F actually represent variants of the same general notion:

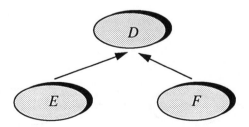

If you recognize this commonality belatedly, the generalization step will enable you to add a common parent class *D*. Here again it would have been preferable to get the hierarchy right the first time around, but late is better than never.

Abstracting and factoring are typical of the process of continuous improvement discussed above. Companies that systematically apply these techniques experience a constant upgrading of the level of abstraction of their library classes, and consequently of the quality of their software investment.

Textbook presentations of the object-oriented method usually introduce inheritance as a process that goes from the general to the specific: you are supposed to derive the highest-level abstractions first, then to add more and more specific variants. If we were all geniuses, this would perhaps be the case.

Or perhaps not, as there is often more than one possible abstraction behind a concrete notion. As a simple example, consider the notion of point in a two-dimensional space (as might arise in graphics software). At least four generalizations are possible:

- Points in arbitrary-dimension space — leading to an inheritance structure where the sisters of class *POINT_2D* will be classes *POINT_3D* and so on.

- Geometrical figures — the other classes in the structure being the likes of *FIGURE*, *RECTANGLE*, *CIRCLE* and so on.

- Polygons — with other classes such as *QUADRANGLE* (four vertices), *TRIANGLE* (three vertices) and *SEGMENT* (two vertices), *POINT* being the special polygon with just one vertex.

- Objects that are entirely determined by two coordinates — the other contenders here being *COMPLEX_NUMBER* and *VECTOR_2D*.

Although some of these generalizations may intuitively be more appealing than others, it is impossible to say in the absolute which one of them is the best. The answer will depend on how your software base evolves and what it will need. So a prudent process in which you sometimes abstract a bit too late, because you waited until you were sure that you had found the most useful path of generalization, may be preferable to one in which you might get too much untested abstraction too soon.

The information hiding part of the object-oriented method helps make sure that belated abstracting and factoring do not harm existing client software. Consider again the above schematic cases, but with a typical client class added to the picture:

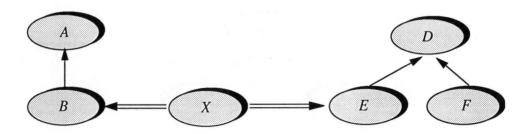

When B gets abstracted into A, or the features of E get factored with those of F into D, a class X that is a client of B or E (on the picture it is a client of both) will in most cases not feel any effect from the change. The ancestry of a class — the inheritance structure that leads to it — does not affect its clients if they are simply applying the features of the class on entities of the corresponding type. In other words, if X uses B and E as suppliers under the scheme

$b1$: B; $e1$: E;

...

$b1$.some_feature_of_B;

...

$e1$.some_feature_of_E

then X is unaffected by any re-parenting of B or E arising from abstracting or factoring.

From a project management perspective this observation means that in many cases the producers (the people working on making the software investment more reusable, either within a project or as part of the reusability group in charge of the library) can quietly carry out their generalization work without disturbing the consumer part of the business (the developers whose classes rely on an earlier iteration of the reusable components).

THE ROLE OF GENERALIZATION

Although generalization is clearly essential for any organization preoccupied with reuse, it is not infrequent, for people who are introduced to the cluster model, to react by criticizing the presence of a separate generalization step: "Why do we need a specific step? Should we not instead apply reusability concerns throughout the construction process?".

Such a comment mistakes a necessary condition for a sufficient one. To obtain reusable software, it is indeed necessary to instill the culture of reusability into your company; but it is dangerous to believe that this will be sufficient.

The short-term pressures — the need to deliver something that works now, satisfying today's requirements rather than future variations — are so strong that without an officially planned generalization step developers are constantly tempted to settle for specific techniques that make it possible to go forward, even if they are not reusable; and management is constantly tempted, once given a first answer to some software need, to transfer the developers to the next task without giving them an opportunity to improve the solution to the current one.

The only way to counter these pressures is to reserve an official step of the lifecycle for generalization, guaranteeing that long-term reusability concerns are not forgotten in the whirlwind of day-to-day constraints. Then, whatever shortcuts a project may have to take in the heat of the moment, some time and resources will be available to clean up your act once you have met the immediate needs.

The traditional, waterfall-based approach includes neither any incentive for generalization in the method nor any room for the corresponding step in the lifecycle model. This is because all the criteria for evaluating success are biased towards the short term: a program element is deemed satisfactory if it works — if it correctly fulfils its specification, is efficient enough, and meets any other project requirements. Why then would the developers continue working on it? Some managers indeed dismiss such extra effort as unneeded or even harmful perfectionism; from a short-term project management perspective, it lowers productivity since it increases the cost for no immediately visible improvement to the product.

Only in a software process emphasizing long-term concerns — the culture of reusability — will it be clear that a program element that works may still warrant further work, since it might be too context-specific to serve again in future developments. To justify the presence of a generalization step in the lifecycle model, you need this long-term perspective.

These observations show once again the need to treat the a priori and a posteriori policies as complementary rather than contradictory. To get reusable components, you must make the concern for reuse pervasive in all phases of the software development process, not only in the generalization step. But instilling the reusability culture, if necessary, is not sufficient because of the short-term pressures of the corporate world. Even with the best of intentions, even if reusability is part of the goals at every step in the process, you will also need the extra step of generalization, during which reusability is the *only* concern.

GENERALIZATION AND THE LIBRARY

There remains to clarify the relationship between generalization and the reusability policy. As defined earlier in this chapter, this policy states the existence of a library, and defines the criteria for accepting candidate components into the library. The library extends across individual projects; its scope is the entire organization. But we also saw the need for a generalization step in each project, meant to derive components. Who then is responsible for defining what becomes a component: the reusability manager (custodian of the library) or individual project managers (promoters of generalization)?

Here too the answer will be: both. As with the nature-nurture debate, both sets of efforts are necessary, but neither is sufficient by itself:

  • The components coming out of a project, even after generalization, may not yet be context-free enough for reuse by other projects. Even if they are, they still need project-independent qualification; this is the task of the people in charge of the library.

  • The library group by itself lacks the advantage of application projects: access to a source of potential components derived from the company's actual developments.

So the process should be in two steps. Each project, through generalization, derives candidate components. When they are judged good enough for reuse on a broader scale, the project submits them to the library group. This is where the qualification process takes place; as noted earlier, getting acceptance will often require a few iterations, as the candidate components may have to go through one or more rounds of uplifting before they meet the library's acceptance criteria.

THE EVOLUTION OF THE LIBRARY

When a component gets accepted into the library, a change of ownership takes place. The component no longer belongs to the project; it has been taken over by the library.

For the project, this is good news, of course; as mentioned at the beginning of this chapter (see point 2 in the table of page 106), one of the advantages of reusability is that you can rely on someone else to take care of maintenance. Once a component becomes part of the library, the reuse group is entrusted with its future evolution. (This will require from the original developers the discipline of using the common version, rather than continuing to develop their own variants; see "THE DISCIPLINE OF REUSABILITY", page 128.)

This process of ownership transfer is one of the characteristic properties of the culture of reusability. It provides one more justification for the advice of setting the stakes high for component acceptance (the Library Entry Principle, page 114): if you are the reusability manager, you will be in charge of maintaining accepted components; so you had better make sure that what you accept will be of good quality.

If the process is successful, the number of components in the library will grow and with it the work that is necessary to keep them up to date: fixing bugs reported by reusers, providing requested extensions, porting to new platforms. This means that the library must have proper resources at its disposal.

Here it becomes apparent that the word *library* is not fully accurate to describe the intended concept — a company's official repertoire of approved reusable software components. Libraries in the non-software sense of the term, those containing shelves where books accumulate dust, are static repertoires; except for the occasional trip to the bindery, a library book will not change. Software components, in contrast, may change; in fact, most of them *must* change since in the software world what does not change usually does not take long to die of oblivion or obsolescence. So the people in charge of the library should not be called librarians, as the conservation part of their job is accessory; they are in fact software developers, and might perhaps receive the (somewhat pompous) job title *reusability engineers*. This holds a lesson for management:

> **LIBRARY EVOLUTION PRINCIPLE**
>
> Treat the library as a software project.

What distinguishes the library project is that instead of being directly dedicated to the company's customers it supports them indirectly by helping the company's other projects. But its other characteristics are those of a normal project — not of a book library.

FUNDING FOR REUSABILITY

The various techniques described in this chapter for promoting the cause of reusable software will require some resources. The investment should be reasonable — we are really talking of adding a few percent to the normal costs of software development — and should repay itself handsomely through the savings and extra quality that reusable components will bring to the company's project; but it must come from somewhere.

We must consider two aspects: funding generalization within each project; and funding the library, especially now that we have identified it as becoming a software project.

For generalization, the budget will come from each project's own resources. Upper management may have to exert some pressure here to make sure everyone follows the rules. A selfish, cynical and ambitious project manager (assuming such exist in your company) might be reluctant at first: after all, the goal of generalization is to grow, out of the current project, reusable components that may help *other* projects, including those whose managers are also in the race for the next higher-level management position. Here the software technology chief must ensure that everyone understands the benefits of reuse (for example that the first beneficiary of generalization will in fact be the original project, for revisions and enhancements of its own product) and, even more importantly in a less-than-angelic world, create a level-playing field. The obligations and benefits must be the same for all projects.

What about funding for the library? There is no universal answer. The library is a company-wide, project-independent effort; large American and European companies, which editorials in business magazines (but not their financial report pages) regularly lambast for having their eyes set on next quarter's return, are not known for their propensity to fund such activities lavishly.

One possible technique is to levy a duty — the **reusability tax** — on software projects, as a compensation for the projects' right to use the library's components. The reusability tax comes in the form of a small percentage (one or two percent seems right) of each project's budget. It is a tax, not a fee; in the same way that you cannot ask for a refund of the portion of your personal taxes that went to the police on the grounds that you did not get mugged last year, the project has to pay the reuse tax whether it uses reusable components or not. This can be understood as an encouragement to reuse.

The tax idea may be pursued further. With the strict library acceptance criteria implied by the Library Entry principle, a project that manages to get some of its own components accepted into the library should receive direct benefits from this success. The project has presumably taken advantage of previous contributions to the library, for which it has paid the reusability tax, and now it is contributing back. Hence the idea of organizing the reusability tax in a way that recalls a European-style *Value-Added-Tax*: every project has to pay the reusability tax; those who are able to make a contribution of their own will receive a partial refund.

THE DISCIPLINE OF REUSABILITY

Before closing on the topic of reusability it is important to examine a potential obstacle to reuse and how to overcome it. The reason why this obstacle has not come up earlier in this discussion is that it can only arise after a reusability policy has already achieved some initial successes.

When projects start reusing software components, the risk exists that, pleased as they may be with the results, they will see needs for extensions or adaptations, and will start modifying the components rather than sticking with the official library versions.

Making the components available in source form increases the temptation, but even with binary components developers may add "wrappers" that extend the component's functionality.

The risk is particularly clear with the process described in this chapter for combining nature and nurture: a project that has had some its generalization-derived components accepted into the library may not have quite completed, emotionally at least, the transfer of ownership studied earlier. If the developers find a need for improvement, they may be tempted to take care of it themselves, rather than asking the library group which is now in charge of the component.

Such temptations are dangerous. Before you have had the time to think about it, you may end up with two or more incompatible variants of what used to be a single product.

> In our own work at ISE, where we have drawn such tremendous benefits from reusability, this is the only negative effect that we have encountered: cases (fortunately only two or three serious ones in ten years of developing reusable software) in which, because the manager was not looking carefully enough and circumstances were pressing, someone took a reusable component and started to adapt it in ways that made it diverge from the evolution of the rest of the product.

The inevitable awakening is always painful, as you have no choice but to stop evolution and merge back the straying streams — tedious work that brings no new functionality, detracts you from more constructive efforts, and should never have been necessary if everyone had been more disciplined.

This risk of divergence is a consequence of the very success of a reusability policy: consumers have become so addicted to their reusable components that they cannot wait to make them do more. But unless it is properly handled it can damage that success: let too many variants blossom, and you do not have a library any more. So the project manager must be vigilant in preaching discipline here.

In the successful implementation of a reusability policy, only at that stage do we have an opportunity for shifting attention — just for once — from the producers to the consumers.

EXERCISE: WHAT ARE THESE PEOPLE DOING WRONG?

To help you test and apply your understanding of the ideas developed in this chapter, here is an exercise based on a comment from a participant at a seminar that I gave in Melbourne (Australia) on some of the topics of this book.

That participant had previously attended a presentation by representatives of a major multinational corporation — a household name (but not a computer company), which shall remain nameless here. Someone in that company's upper management seems to be a bright-eyed reusability enthusiast, and here is how I was told they are going about it:

> *He* [the speaker at the company's presentation] *said that their reuse policy was based on the idea that they would aim never to write another line of detail code, and so the classes developed by the client accounts team would go into their reuse library, and subsequent teams would be directed to use those classes. He seemed to recognize that the first team would not necessarily do a good job, but that they would get better with time, and didn't really explain how he thought that subsequent teams would get good reuse from this. It may be that he envisaged revising the library as subsequent problems were identified, but he didn't say so.*

His real problem might be uncertainty about who has responsibility for creating a good class library. He made a number of contradictory remarks. For example he said that some businesses are banning inheritance because it leads to uncontrolled expansion of the hierarchy and loss of control by management. That doesn't seem to fit in with his hopes for the work of the first team, either. I think I can certainly say that he saw reuse as a consumer problem, and that he recognized that these consumers would be forced to reuse work that was designed in the context of one specific application and without a firm methodology for ensuring that the work would be of a sufficiently general nature for other uses.

He did say that subsequent programmers wanting to write fresh code for things already in the reuse library would have to justify their request. I suppose that is the best indication of where they feel responsibility lies. He definitely had a strong bias towards management functions. He said that the prime job of the company was to get the business functions right and ignore the technical details. I don't think of technical things as "details".

Based on the above description, the exercise requires that you answer the following questions:

- Are "the details" relevant to the company's business?

- Is the library going to be of good quality?

- When developers are forced to use that library, is the resulting software going to be of good quality?

- If the answer to the previous question is no, who will be blamed?

- (Optional question for extra credit) In this company, what will be the conventional wisdom about object technology and reusability one year after the above policy has been put into place?

BIBLIOGRAPHY

Bertrand Meyer: *Reusable Software: The Base Object-Oriented Component Libraries**, Prentice Hall, 1994.

> Presents a set of design principles for building quality libraries, and their application to a set of fundamental libraries — about 150 classes — covering data structures, algorithms, lexical analysis and parsing.

Ted J. Biggerstaff and Alan J. Perlis, eds.: *Software Reusability*, Addison-Wesley, 1989 (two volumes).

> A collection of articles on various aspects of building reusable software, a few of which apply O-O ideas.

James C. McKim, Jr.: *KISSing, the Joy of Stacks, and USSR*, Guest Editorial, *Journal of Object-Oriented Programming*, vol. 7, no. 4, July-August 1994, pages 6-8.

> A short article that calls the reader's attention to the usefulness of the stack example to understand abstraction and other object-oriented principles.

7

The manager's role, 1: Fundamentals

A large software project is more similar to a symphony orchestra than to a string quartet: there must be a leader. This chapter and the next two examine the role of that leader — the project manager.

In software the term "manager" is not without some ambiguity. The responsibility can be purely administrative; it can be purely technical; or it can be some combination of the two. There are almost as many situations as companies — almost as many, in fact, as projects. This diversity explains why the discussion has been split into three parts. The present chapter studies the components of the manager's job that apply to all cases. The next chapter explores the case of managers who have a strong technical background in software, whether they contribute some of the software themselves (the Pinchas Zukerman style) or prefer to remain just managers. The third chapter in this series will study the special situation of a manager whose background is not in software.

The major managerial responsibilities studied in the rest of this chapter are summarized by the following list:

> **MANAGER RESPONSIBILITIES**
>
> **Risk Manager**
>
> **Deadline keeper**
>
> **Interface with the rest of the world**
>
> **Protector of the team's sanity**

RISK MANAGER

The principal role of the project manager is to predict, avoid and handle risk. Risk in a software project comes from many possible sources:

- Unexpected technical difficulties.

- Late delivery of necessary hardware.

- Bugs in externally acquired software, such as operating systems, compilers, development tools.

- Unavailability of key project members (resignation, illness or other absence, reassignment to other projects).

- Company politics.

- Competitive pressure.

For the most part, the techniques for handling such situations are not specific to software. They involve being enough of a pessimist to imagine the worst possible situations even when everything seems to go well; identifying the critical path (the steps on which everything else depends) early in the process; and devising alternative policies well before the primary policies have failed.

DEADLINE KEEPER

The outside world will expect the manager to announce deadlines and stick to them. Observing deadlines is tricky business in software development because of the uncertainties that cloud most software projects.

Software cost models (such as COCOMO, described in Barry Boehm's book cited on page 59) can help; but they work best for situations in which there have been many projects of a similar nature before, resulting in the accumulation of extensive cost data, directly applicable to the current effort — not your average object-oriented project.

INTERFACE WITH THE REST OF THE WORLD

The project leader serves as primary interface to the rest of the world, in particular upper management, marketing and customers. This is a delicate role, especially when the team is using a new technology which may not be fully clear to these other actors. The duties of the manager here include:

- Making sure that the expectations on both sides are realistic.

- Ensuring that the development team has the full support of the rest of the company.

- Ensuring that the development team is aware of the business priorities and receptive to the needs of the company and its customers.

PROTECTOR OF THE TEAM'S SANITY

Part of the manager's interface role is to protect the team from unwanted interference. Here there is a fine line to walk. On the one hand, you must prevent the developers from going into stand-alone mode, where they become obsessed with internal technical details and forget the underlying business problems. But you also know that software development requires concentration and some protection from the vagaries of daily company life.

Some of the consequences of this role will be probed further in the discussion of the special dangers that threaten non-technical managers (see "PANIC CRISES", page 150).

CRISIS REMEDY

Project X, or cluster Y of the project, is in trouble. Deadlines are being missed; designs get changed; nothing seems to come out. Developers are depressed; those who need the results — other projects or clusters, customers, higher management — are worried.

Because of your reputation as a great project manager, you are asked for help. What do you do?

Although each such situation is special, the following advice is applicable in most cases:

> ### LIM (LESS IS MORE) CRISIS REMEDY PRINCIPLE
>
> To get a project back on track, consider *removing* people and functionality.

The LIM principle may appear counter-intuitive at first. A crisis context seems to encourage adding people to the project: everyone wants the project to do *more*; and because you are being called to the rescue in a difficult situation, you may indeed obtain more people if you ask. So the temptation is there.

But consider why the project is in trouble. In most such cases that I have seen, some (or often all) of the following conditions applied:

1 • Goals were poorly defined (typically, six months into the project, someone starts to ask "What are we really trying to do?" and no one can agree on the answer).

2 • Goals were too ambitious.

3 • Not everyone in the team was up to speed.

Adding more people is not going to make things better. This is the so-called Brooks's law (for the book's reference, see page 71): *Adding more people to a late project makes it later.* Famous as this quote is, managers often forget it, since it is so much easier to add people.

The LIM principle goes further than Brooks's law by stating that in many cases you should not only refrain from adding to the team but actually remove team members.

Why? Consider in particular problems 2 and 3 above (ambitious goals, team competence). In every situation of this kind that I have seen, the team consisted of two groups: (A) a productive kernel of effective people; and (B) a set of less competent developers. This is usually because problem 3 was a consequence of problem 2: the scope defined for the project was too broad, so management took the easy road — just adding people. But then you do not find experienced and well-trained developers (especially *object-oriented* developers) just like that, so the level of the additional people was in some cases so-so. As a result, not only do group B people produce little; they also detract group A people from doing their own job! The Law of the Bad Apple applies in such cases: everyone tends to slow down to the level of the least productive participants.

Adding more people would only make the situation worse.

The remedy, then, is to face reality: at this stage it is probably impossible to get the full expected functionality in the near future. The solution is a concerted attack on both problem 2 and problem 3:

> ### APPLYING THE LIM PRINCIPLE
>
> Keep only the core group of most effective developers.
>
> Keep only the core subset of essential functionality.

You must wield your axe in both areas. Cutting the less effective part of the group will free the others to do their work and do it well. Cutting the less important or more baroque part of the functionality is required if you want to be able to provide the essential parts.

This approach assumes some courage, but it is the inescapable route in such a situation. You will be criticized for both decisions:

- The decision to remove some people from the project will make some think that you have gone crazy. Even in normal circumstances project managers seldom give up team members, as team size is a measure of status and power; but in addition you are removing people in a project that is proceeding *too slowly*? Must be time for some rest.

- The decision to remove some functionality will start everyone screaming. We can't do without a drag-and-drop interface! The marketing guys have already promised constant database integrity to Cresus-Midas! It has to run on a 2-MB 286 too!

But such criticism should not intimidate you. Those who think you should not let developers go are welcome to include them in their own projects. As to the screaming about sacrificed functionality, the answer is easy, in the form of a multiple-choice questionnaire: Do you prefer: (1) The essential functionality, four months from now. (2) All of the functionality, four centuries from now. (3) None of the above. (Check one box only.) This should give the screamers something to think about.

The ingredients for making a development team succeed are no big mystery. The developers must feel that everyone of their colleagues on the team is competent. They must believe that their assigned task is realistic. They must be free to apply their time to this task, free of distractions — such as meetings, politics, training novices, making up for the messes produced by less competent team members. And, more important than anything else (although partly a consequence of the other conditions) they must see results coming out regularly — where, as we saw in an earlier chapter, the only really significant results are elements of *code* that actually run.

By focusing on the right objective with the right group of people equipped with the tools and techniques of object technology, you stand a good chance of ensuring these conditions and restoring the morale of the team members and their faith in the project. After a while some code will start to appear again. It will perhaps not be much initially as compared to the magnitude of the task, but it will be running code, and good-quality code. Enough to show everyone — most importantly the team developers, but also the critics and the screamers — that you mean business and are going to produce something serious.

Once the project is back on track and has started to produce usable results, it will always be possible to consider the removed functionality again. At that time you might also consider adding people: a robust product and project can afford having a few more developers, working at the periphery to add the extra bells and whistles that might enlarge the product's market appeal. But until then — until the core of the software is ready — including non-essential features and non-essential people would be suicidal.

HARDWARE RESOURCES

For human resources, more can be less. Is this true for other resources, in particular hardware and software?

No. Here the situation is fundamentally different: software developers should be given all the tools they need. Stinginess is foolishness.

The extraordinary evolution of the computer industry has made it possible to treat powerful hardware facilities as a commodity. There is no excuse for letting software developers fight with insufficient resources, for example by making tape copies of files for lack of disk space, or sitting in front of their consoles waiting for a compilation to finish because the CPU is not fast enough.

If there is an area where the manager should not skimp, this is it. Yet one routinely sees managers who do not hesitate about hiring more team members but will refuse an extra disk or a faster workstation to those people already on the team.

The goal is not luxury but simply enabling developers to do their jobs properly. Putting on a developer's desk a hardware-software mix that costs half of the developer's yearly salary already goes a long way.

THE SOFTWARE DEVELOPER'S BILL
OF RESOURCE RIGHTS

• Every software developer shall have a personal development workstation.

• Every software developer's workstation shall have at least 32 Megabytes of memory, at least one Gigabyte of disk space, a graphical screen, a modern operating system, an advanced graphical development environment, good text processing tools.

• Every software developer's workstation shall have a CPU offering at least 50 MIPS of computing power.

• Every software developer shall have access to both internal and external e-mail as well as to network news (for technical groups), FTP and network browsing tools.

In the statement of this principle, the figures given (for speed and space) represent minimum values applicable at the time this book was being written. It will not take long before some of them appear too timid.

Let us look at the various requirements. The personal development workstation is a clear necessity: the time when programmers had to fight for resources on a time-shared system is past. 32 Megabytes of memory is the minimum required by many development tools; soon 64 will be considered indispensable. As for disk space, the price in the US went below 1 dollar per megabyte as this book was being written, and the downward progression is continuing. Programmers need space; 1 Gigabyte is the minimum for comfort, and there is no excuse for denying them this $1,000 or less investment.

The graphical screen makes it possible to use modern development environments. People in the software business are so opinionated about operating systems that I cowardly prefer (for fear of offending someone) not to be more specific about what I mean by "modern operating system", but you should be able to interpret this phrase for yourself — and almost all the major OS are catching up quickly anyway. Many developers will need to write documentation, internal or external, and modern text processing tools supporting both text and graphics must be available for that purpose; the development workstation can double up as a text processing workstation. Most people these days will want the text processing facilities to have an interface of the so-called WYSIWYG (what you see is what you get) type, compatible with what they expect from the software development environment.

MIPS (Million Instructions Per Second) is a measure of CPU speed — notoriously imprecise, but giving at least an order of magnitude. Software developers need speed; waiting for a compilation to complete is not a good use of their time.

Electronic communication tools are becoming increasingly important to software development:

• Electronic mail is indispensable to get answers to technical questions, send elements of code, design or specification, and more generally as the basic medium of technical discussion, for managers as well as developers (see "ABOUT COMMUNICATION TOOLS", page 147).

- Network news means access to a precious information resource: discussion groups on many subjects from programming languages (*comp.lang.eiffel*, *comp.lang.smalltalk* and many others), operating systems (such as *comp.os.ms-windows*) and compiling techniques (*comp.compilers*) to advanced computer science topics (*comp. specification*) and legal issues.

Network news is a tremendous and essentially free source of information, from which almost all projects can benefit. You may want to control its use, limiting it for example to the *comp* (computers) hierarchy, since it is unlikely that groups such as *rec.food.drink.beer* and others in the *rec* (recreation) hierarchy are essential to your project; but the benefits provided by legitimate uses more than compensate for the risk that someone will occasionally abuse the facilities.

Beyond mail and news, electronic communication tools include FTP (File Transfer Protocol), through which you can transfer files from thousands of sites worldwide that provide countless free tools, and browsing facilities such as Mosaic enabling you to explore sites worldwide, using hypertext techniques which take you from site to site on the so-called *World-Wide Web* (WWW) as you mouse-click on keywords of interest. Although these mechanisms have been widely available for a short time only, they are gaining thousands of new converts daily; companies that are shunning them for any reason (ignorance, conservatism, misplaced security concerns) are depriving themselves and their projects of extraordinary opportunities.

Since the author's company is of course a card-carrying member of all such electronic communities, this may be the right place to give his WWW access information and electronic mail:

Web home page: *http://www.tools.com*
Electronic mail address: *meyer@tools.com*

BIBLIOGRAPHY

Tom de Marco and Tim Lister: *Peopleware*, Dorset Publishing, New York, 1988.

A useful discussion of the human side of software project management. Includes harangues for managers who do not understand the special needs of programmers (private workspace, no interruptions). Focuses on helping managers make a team "jell". The book unfortunately succumbs at times to the temptation of demagoguery: it downplays the tough decisions that every project faces, and instead advises managers to relax and be nice, as if software development and project management were all about smiling and letting programmers work from 9 to 5. Yet this is a good discussion of the specificity of the software profession, and in particular we often recommend it as background reading for non-technical project managers (whose role will be studied in chapter 9).

8

The manager's role, 2: Technical manager

In addition to the duties that fall on all managers, a technical manager (also called "project leader" in the rest of this chapter) is responsible for several tasks: division into clusters; integration; demo keeping; method enforcement; mentoring; pre-official quality assurance. Let us look at the details.

THE MANAGER AS CLUSTER DIVIDER

The cluster model for the construction of a software system covered in chapter 3 (see the figure on page 53) includes an initial step labeled "Division into clusters", devoted to the identification of the system's major units. This step is the responsibility of the project leader. Other people will help, but it is the project leader, as the most senior person on the team, who should carry the primary burden.

There is no "methodology" for identifying the clusters. Experience with previous projects (which is of course a primary criterion for being appointed project leader in the first place) will provide the basic ideas: if you have done a compiler project before, for example, you will not have trouble identifying such basic clusters as lexical aspects, parsing aspects, semantics, optimization and so on. Familiarity with libraries of reusable components, both internally developed and available from the market, is important, as some clusters may well be based on existing libraries or even be entirely covered by the components of such a library.

More generally, the cluster divider must have a high-level view of the system, an ability for systems reasoning, solid industry experience, and a talent for making bright decisions that integrate other people's advice — the kind of qualities that we expect to find in a good technical project manager.

THE MANAGER AS INTEGRATOR

Once the clusters have been started and the process starts turning out results, one of the primary tasks of the project manager is **cluster integration.**

Integration is the process of putting together all the clusters of a project. It provides an opportunity to check that each cluster meets the assumptions that the others have made about it, and of correcting any inconsistency detected in the process.

Integration will normally proceed smoothly in a well-managed and well-staffed O-O project. But it needs to be done carefully because the concurrent engineering nature of the cluster model raises the risk of clusters diverging — becoming incompatible with each other. As noted in the discussion of the lifecycle, the method helps: information hiding protects clusters against internal changes in other clusters on which they depend; and Design by Contract makes such dependencies explicit by encouraging designers to state what each module offers to others and expects from others. These techniques, however, only reduce the divergence risk; they do not eliminate it.

The only solution is a pragmatic one: do not give clusters the time to diverge; integrate them frequently. More precisely:

> ### INTEGRATION PRINCIPLE
>
> The time between successive integrations of all of a project's cluster should never be more than four weeks.

Finding the right frequency requires a tradeoff: if you integrate too frequently, you may disrupt the progress of individual clusters; if you procrastinate, you increase the risk that some clusters will become incompatible, forcing you to go through a painful reconciliation process. At a technology buildup stage, when you are repeatedly changing some fundamental clusters used by many others, you should integrate more frequently; in more stable states you can afford to wait a little longer from one integration to the next. But in all cases experience suggests that the four week period given in the Integration Principle is the limit beyond which you are endangering the success of your project.

At ISE the average has been about one integration every two weeks. We almost never wait more than three weeks (we did this a few times in the past, and usually regretted it); at times of frequent change, and just before a major new release, we integrate every week. The general trend in our recent work has in fact been to bring down the average to one week, even in the absence of any immediately compelling incentive; one of the reasons for having such frequent integrations is to make sure, with the help of the proper tools for version and configuration management, that each integration adds to the project's baseline a precise record of what was done, including detailed comments about the changes that were made since the previous integration and the rationale behind each one of these changes. If you wait more than a week, some of this information will simply not be available — the developers may have forgotten why exactly they made a particular decision. Six months later, when you rummage through the software to try to correct some new problem, you may regret not having this information available as part of the record.

With good tools and an experienced development group integration becomes a fast and relatively painless process, so the argument cited earlier against frequent integrations (disrupting the progress of cluster development) loses its strength.

Several reasons suggest that a technical project manager should treat integration as a personal responsibility, even if other team members will assist (especially in a large project) in carrying out the task:

- Integration requires understanding the entire project.

- To be done properly, integration will also require in-depth knowledge of the object-oriented method.

- Integration implies communication with all the teams in the project.

- Integration is one of the checkpoints for spotting mistakes and improper design or implementation decisions.

To these must be added a practical reason: the person in charge of integration is also the best equipped to maintain a *current demonstration version* of the project's eventual product. This concept is sufficiently important to justify separate examination.

THE MANAGER AS DEMO KEEPER

As more time and resources are spent on a project, various outside parties — higher management, financial backers, important customers or prospects who "happen" to be visiting the area, members of the marketing department, managers and developers from other projects who will need to rely on the results of the current one — will become increasingly restive and will want to see something that runs. This means that someone must put together a temporary version of the software under construction, which incorporates as many elements as possible so as to produce a good impression on people who see a demonstration.

In the constantly changing environment of a software project, the task of maintaining a reasonably up-to-date demonstration available at all times is one more burden; developers are often reluctant to take care of it, as they feel it detracts from the really serious aspects of the development for the sake of satisfying short-term requests. As with integration, to which it is closely related, several reasons suggest that the project manager should treat this task as a personal responsibility:

- The manager is the one who deals with the outside world anyway, interacting with higher management, marketing and other partners, and shielding the developers from the resulting pressures.

- The manager is the one who must know, as early as possible, if a mistake has been made.

- The manager is the one who must decode the developer's vague assessments of progress — "it's almost done" — and translate them from the realm of feelings to the realm of reality. Uttered by some people, "almost done" means done; coming from others, it means 20% done. Nothing will help evaluate such assessments better than an attempt to include the modules into a system that runs, however modest and temporary.

All this suggests complementing the manager's role as Integrator by the role of Demo Keeper.

How justified, by the way, is the developers' frequent contention, mentioned above, that preparing demos takes time away from the "real work" and delays the project? It is not without merit but must be taken with a grain of salt. Although short-term disruptions can indeed be damaging, especially if they occur often, many a project leader has also discovered the positive results that can be achieved by the need to demonstrate something next week. This is a good opportunity to tie up a few loose ends and complete modules that in theory were finished but in practice did not quite work yet.

This positive influence of the need to get serious for an impending demo could be called the **demo effect**. In software folklore, of course, "demo effect" means something else: a variant of the so-called Murphy's law, meaning a mysterious tendency of apparently robust systems to fail just when you are showing them to someone important.

The new form of demo effect has its limitations. If a certain milestone is several weeks away, no amount of short-term pressure will miraculously enable you to reach it in two days. But for something that is internally ready or almost ready, the extra work that follows from a request to put it in presentable form is seldom wasted:

- Cleaning up modules to enable the production of a demo version also makes them usable by other components of the development.

- In addition, there is the psychological effect: in a long-haul project, where it is so easy for everyone to get depressed by the knowledge of how much remains to be done, a successful demo which impresses a few unbiased outsiders by the quality of what has *already* been done is the best known morale booster.

- Finally, the ability to produce early runnable versions provides a good opportunity to spot flaws or omissions that could be much harder to correct if they were detected only later; this does not delay the development but speeds it up.

THE MANAGER AS METHOD ENFORCER

To build a system the object-oriented way means to follow a precise method, including both high-level principles (abstraction, information hiding, proper use of inheritance and the like) and many specific style rules. Everyone in the project should understand the principles and the rules.

Even with the best of intentions, however, developers may be tempted to stray away from these rules under everyday pressures. It is the manager's responsibility to ensure that this does not happen (and to grant exemptions when appropriate).

This task is consistent with the manager's role as integrator: integration, which depends so heavily on module interface standards, is an ideal opportunity to monitor observance of the rules and take any corrective action as may be needed.

MENTOR AND CRITIC

A project leader who is not just a manager but also a senior engineer will play several informal roles along with the official ones.

Not all team members will be equally at ease with object technology. They must all be properly trained, but training by itself is not always sufficient; a technical project leader can complement it by serving as a mentor. This may involve a bit of hand-holding, much encouragement, and occasional help in applying what has been taught: in what class should I include this feature? Should I absolutely reuse this library class, or will it be better if I write my own variant? Is it OK to have such a flat inheritance hierarchy, or should I try to introduce more intermediate levels? Is multiple inheritance overkill here?

Another role is related to the task of method enforcement discussed above. If a formal quality assurance process is in place, in particular if every piece of software produced by the development team must be approved by a separate qualification team, it is preferable to avoid experiencing too many rejections in this process. The project leader can act as the first quality controller, taking a look at submissions before they go out to the qualification team, and detecting serious deficiencies in time. Rather than risking a formal rejection, and the damage that it will probably cause to both project schedule and developer ego, it is better in such a case to ask the developer to work further on the product before submitting it officially.

These aspects of the manager's role are facilitated by the abstraction mechanisms of the object-oriented method, which enable a competent person to examine a chunk of object-oriented software, get quickly familiar with its essential properties, and focus on some of its aspects while ignoring irrelevant details.

CHIEF PROGRAMMER TEAMS

If you are familiar with the classical software engineering literature, you may have noted some analogies between the above ideas and an approach which had its hour of fame in the nineteen-seventies: chief programmer teams.

The Chief Programmer Team is a team organization applicable to developments that proceed in a traditional top-down fashion; it is based on a project leader, the chief programmer, who as the name suggests is competent as a technical developer. The chief programmer, aside from managing the development, should personally write the most crucial software elements, those at the top of the top-down hierarchy. Chief programmer teams are strongly structured, with a hierarchical organization mirroring the tree-like structure of a top-down program decomposition.

These aspects of chief programmer teams do not transpose to object-oriented development, which is a bottom-up approach emphasizing reusability and extendibility. Nor do they fit well with the decomposition into clusters, and more generally with the cluster model.

Even in a traditional context, many projects that have attempted to apply Chief Programmer Team discovered the obvious: the demands that a large software project puts on its manager are so heavy that it is unrealistic to base the development on the assumption that the manager will personally write key parts of the software. This would mean making the schedule hinge on the manager's ability to perform technical work that, by nature, requires full-time concentration. Not the best way to minimize risk.

In spite of all these limitations the notion of Chief Programmer Team still provides a few important ideas. In particular, the view that the project leader should not be *just* a manager, but should be technically savvy and ready to take the plunge into development when needed, is as important today (and as subversive in some companies) as it was when Chief Programmer Teams were first publicized.

The difference with the Chief Programmer Team approach is that in a large project the project plan will not assign any parts of the development to the team leader. But this is not the same thing as saying that the leader should never write software. Opportunities for occasional intervention abound: adding some "glue" to put together a demo; temporarily substituting for a team member who has left or is unable to work; taking over when you find out that someone has messed up some crucial part of the job.

A project leader's demonstrated ability to program when needed can also change, for the better, the atmosphere in the project; developers will have more respect for someone whom they feel to be technically as competent as them (or preferably more competent). This change reflects the subtle difference that exists between the terms *project leader* and *manager,* even though this chapter and the two enclosing ones use them interchangeably. To talk about a manager reflects an "us and them" view where the developers belong to one profession and the managers to another. A manager who is not afraid to roll up shirt sleeves and have dirty hands once in a while may succeed in being viewed more as one of "us". Although this situation is not without some dangers, as will be seen in the next chapter (see "THE DEBUGGER THAT WOULD HAVE COST AN ARM AND A LEG", page 151), it can help the emergence of a true team spirit.

In the sixteenth century, the philosopher Michel de Montaigne, on being presented an American Indian freshly brought in from the newly discovered continent, asked him what the privileges of a chieftain were in his people, to which the answer was: "He marches first to war". (Four centuries later, the ethnographer Clause Lévi-Strauss, posed the same question to an Amazonian chief, and got the same answer.) Developers, too, will prefer a marching chief to an armchair general.

BIBLIOGRAPHY

F. Terry Baker: *Chief Programmer Team Management of Production Programming*, in *IBM Systems Journal*, volume 11, number 1, 1971, pages 56-73.

An often referenced article that introduced the notion of Chief Programmer Team. The presentation of this notion in Fred Brooks's *The Mythical Man-Month* (see page 71) is more easily availabe today.

9

The manager's role, 3: Non-technical manager

One of the distinctive properties of the software industry, as compared to long-established engineering disciplines, is the number of leadership positions filled by people who do not have a strong technical background in the profession, but were primarily trained as managers without a specific technical focus, or came from other technical specialties such as electronics or physics.

This situation may be ascribed, among other reasons, to the relative youth of our field. Also fostering it is the apparent absence of initial technical barriers: it is easier to acquire a little hands-on experience in programming than in, say, VLSI design; this may delay the realization that becoming an expert is as difficult in either of these fields as it is in the other.

Although software people can sometimes be heard to deplore the presence of non-software specialists at the helm of software endeavors, such a situation is not without its advantages: it can let software development benefit from management experience accumulated in older, better-understood disciplines; and it can help ensure that the users' view does not get forgotten.

In any case we do not need to delve further into the reasons behind this peculiarity of the software field; nor is it very productive to expatiate on whether its benefits outweigh its drawbacks. It is simply part of the reality of our field, and we must take it for granted. But we must also analyze what special requirements it puts on everyone involved — the non-technical managers, and the technical people who work with them.

What makes this question critical is the amount of damage that can happen if the task is not properly performed. It is maddening to see, over and again, intelligent and experienced managers repeat the same mistakes. They do what they should not do, yet they do not do what they could and should do. I hope that the following observations can help a few non-technical managers avoid the usual catastrophes, and help a few software professionals develop a productive relationship with their non-technical bosses.

The first type of advice will cover what not to do — actions that may tempt a manager but are usually counter-productive. Sometimes the best course of action is no action at all. After these negative admonitions the discussion will switch to the positive and describe what special contributions a non-technical manager *can* make in addition to the general duties of all managers.

MEETINGITIS

Like many other arduous professions, management has its occupational diseases. One of the worst hazards associated with the job is a condition known as *meetingitis*.

Although not lethal under ordinary circumstances, meetingitis is highly contagious and places a terrible burden on those closely associated with the sufferer, such as co-workers, family and personal stockbrokers. The early symptoms, most readily observable in a recently promoted manager, are a propensity to call meetings for all kinds of reason or, in the most common strain of the disease, for no reason at all. The sources of the malady are unknown, although some experts have posited a psycho-somatic explanation (*Ur-managerialität*), going back to the hunter-gatherer stage of the species, when the usual way to claim power over a certain territory, it is alleged, was to take hostages.

The damage may be limited as long as the hostages are other managers; trouble begins when the meetings involve programmers. Good software developers do not always take kindly to useful meetings, but they invariably take unkindly to useless meetings. Having ten competent programmers waste an entire morning in a poorly ventilated room wastes more than thirty person-hours, since in many cases not much will get done in the following afternoon. The worst consequence is the pent-up exasperation — "Why don't they just let us do our work?".

The situation can quickly develop into a disaster. The more you take developers away from their job, the less work gets done. Deadlines slip, the manager worries even more, and what then is the reaction? Why, convene a meeting, of course — to which even more people will be summoned for help, including those from the parts of the project that are *still* doing all right, although thanks to the meetings that will not last much longer. Soon everyone will be infected. The more meetings, the more delays; and the more delays, the more meetings.

One of the most important duties of a manager is to help every supervised person spend as much time and energy as possible on what the person does best for the benefit of the company. What a good programmer does best is programming. Meetings are a waste of programmers' time except in the following circumstances:

- A technical meeting called to resolve a specific technical question, provided the participants together have all the elements needed for that solution, and each individual participant has at least one such element to contribute.

- A review meeting called to examine a specific product (analysis, design, implementation, documentation) of the software development process, according to well-defined evaluation criteria, provided there is a good reason for performing such an examination, and no better alternative, such as automatic examination by software tools, is available. In the software engineering literature this is known as an *inspection*.

- A one-on-one performance evaluation meeting.

- A seminar where someone makes a technical presentation.

- A meeting to announce a team's precise goals and objectives for the forthcoming weeks or months.

Effective meetings tend to fall into two categories: top-down and bottom-up. In the top-down variant one person (or sometimes two or three speaking with a single voice) do most of the talking; others can intervene, but mostly to contribute comments or questions. The last two cases in the preceding list belong to this category. In the bottom-up variant, all participants, or a substantial subset, are expected to contribute; this can only work if the number of participants is small. The first two items in the above list belong to this category.

When meetings are justified, they must follow stringent rules. They must be short; most should take less than one hour, and few should ever last more than two. (After two hours attention simply wanes and nothing useful happens.) There must be a precise agenda. It must be clear to every participant what goals the meeting is trying to achieve, so that at the end everyone knows whether these goals have been reached or not.

> Failure to reach the meeting's goals is not necessarily a catastrophe; it is often simply a sign that the solution, if any, can only be found outside of the meeting. In such a case it is preferable to make the situation clear to everyone and cut the meeting at the scheduled time, resisting the natural temptation to ramble on and on.

A meeting must involve a small number of participants— two to five in most cases; meetings of the bottom-up category, in particular, cannot be productive with many participants. A common mistake which can hurt even legitimate meetings is to invite too many people, usually for fear of offending those who are kept out. But such fear is a poor advisor. A meeting should only involve the people whose participation is indispensable; others can be informed and make further contributions through other means.

In every meeting there must be someone in charge of enforcing time constraints and bringing the discussion back on track when necessary. This does not need to be the person with the highest managerial rank, nor (for obvious reasons) should it usually be in the top-down variant be the person who will do most of the talking.

ABOUT COMMUNICATION TOOLS

One of the reasons managers like to convene meetings is that they know the importance of communication. But alternatives to the meeting exist, which will establish communication without the penalties of meetings.

One such alternative is the NMM (the Non-Meeting Meeting): all the casual opportunities afforded by chance encounters in the hallway, around the coffee machine or the water fountain, at the softball game. It is striking to see how many questions can be resolved and how many people can be set back on the right track through informal but focused exchanges of that kind.

Also useful in many cases is electronic mail. Although some managers are still resisting this modern communication vehicle, there is no excuse for such an attitude since E-mail these days can be used by everyone, not just techies. It retains and combines the best aspects of each of the previously available techniques: from face-to-face discussions, instantaneousness and informality; from the telephone, liberation from the tyranny of distance; from postal mail, ability to think over outgoing messages for as long as necessary before sending them, and to read incoming messages at one's leisure; from the fax, guarantee that there is a trace of the communication at both the sending and receiving ends, and ability to forward a received message (to someone else, to your home, to your hotel if you are traveling) without forsaking the original copy; from photocopy, production of as many duplicates as desired; from the printed book, readability and cleanliness of the text, identical for all copies; from computer technology, ease of modification, and integration with other tools such as text editors. And all that in most cases at a cheaper cost than with any other communication mechanism.

Electronic mail works best to discuss specific technical points and to distribute small chunks of information to a small or large group of people. It is a tremendously powerful mode of communication. For managing a software project it has the extra advantage that software developers like it because it is non-disruptive (as opposed to meetings and telephone calls) and integrates naturally with the rest of their work, with which it shares the developer's basic workspace — the screen.

Like anything else, electronic mail has its risks and must be managed properly. A problem of which the manager must be aware results from e-mail's original combination of attributes from verbal and written communication. Like a printed text and unlike a conversation, an e-mail message stays around for every recipient to peruse; but like a spoken remark it is often dispatched quickly and without much advance thinking. The consequences are well known to e-mail veterans: the ease with which people get offended. The "flame wars" that periodically erupt on network discussion groups are typical of this phenomenon.

For the manager, the lesson is clear: every group that uses electronic mail as a common communication mechanism should have strict rules as to what is admissible as contents of e-mail messages. The rules should state that e-mail is reserved for announcements, for sharing information, and for the discussion of specific technical points. They should explicitly forbid any kind of ad hominem attack, and any complaint or whining of a general nature against co-workers, management or the company.

A manager who has discovered the power of electronic mail may at first balk at the idea of exerting such censorship. But it is indispensable, and the manager must be ever vigilant to intervene at the first sign of impropriety. One misguided attack or disgruntled comment, and soon all the network is abuzz with arguments and counter-arguments. All work comes to a halt as team members spend their time honing their spears, dressing their wounds and counting their dead.

What you are censoring as a manager is not disagreement, as electronic mail is perfectly able to support heated debates between widely different views, as long as they remain focused on specific technical points. Neither are you denying that personal conflicts may arise, and that part of the manager's role is to confront and help resolve them. You are simply preventing the use of group e-mail for that purpose, because it is not suited to it.

To deal with personal conflicts, you will have to use other techniques, documented in the generic management literature (assuming you need such advice). And, yes, one of them may be, once in a while, to convene a meeting.

MONDAY MORNING CONSULTING FROM *COMPUTERWEEK*

Together with meetingitis, a typical manager foible is overreaction to the notoriously fickle analyses of the computer press.

ComputerWeek lands on the manager's desk and presently the world comes to an end: a journalist has decreed (with all the authority conferred by a six-month internship) that Microsoft is in and NEXT is out, or maybe that NEXT is in and Microsoft is out. Worse yet, the journalist has talked to a few users and has found that, would you believe it, introducing object technology is not a path strewn with roses. Quick, my telephone! Todd, are you sure we should be doing this? Look at the story about how Sloppy Burger Inc. lost its ketchup in trying to implement objects! Sure we don't want to go back to COBOL, but don't you think we could put something together just by using Lotus Notes and a 4GL?

ComputerWeek (a fictitious name) is used here as a symbol for the specialized press. Old-timers in the field understand the role of these publications — to reflect the buzz and moods of the computer industry — and have learned not to attach too much significance to its fashions and counter-fashions; they know that today's burning topic or product may be tepid tomorrow, cold next week, and gone next month.

Non-technical managers, however, may actually *believe* what they read in *ComputerWeek*. This need not cause too much damage — unless they use such Monday morning sources of wisdom as an excuse to turn the project upside down every Monday afternoon.

180° DEGREE TURNS

The Monday Morning Consulting phenomenon is a special case of a common reaction: the sudden impulse to reverse earlier decisions. Let's drop Unix and go to Windows, replace a database management system by another, revert from a client-server architecture to a centralized system.

The need for dramatic reversals of earlier policies does arise, of course. Part of what characterizes a good manager is indeed the courage to admit failures, cut one's losses, and restart with a better plan. But such a decision should not be taken lightly: it requires a technically sound analysis, showing that the present policy is flawed — that is to say, will probably lead to failure if continued — and that the proposed replacement is better. The analysis should also take into account the effect of disrupting the current process. Only after having weighed these various elements can you make an informed choice.

In some cases the choice will be to rescind the previous policy; in others the conclusion will be that it is better to leave good enough alone, and that (say) the ABC database management system will do the job even though it might have been better, six months earlier, to choose XYZ instead.

But nothing is worse than a succession of wide swings of the rudder, not backed by a proof that the previous decision was flawed. They will leave the team confused, demoralized, and unwilling in the future to commit to *any* policy for fear of another reversal.

PANIC CRISES

Rudder swings may be a consequence of yet another common managerial plague: failure to protect the project from external crises or, worse yet, amplification of these crises.

Communication between a project and the outside world, especially higher echelons of management, is not always smooth. When playing golf with another CEO, our CEO heard that everyone now is using object-oriented databases: why are we still relational? A major customer threatens to go to the competition unless we provide an intermediate release now, disrupting all our plans. A large shareholder complains that we are not focusing on "industry-standard" tools. The legal department, which has just completed the acquisition of company P, insists that we develop "synergy" by using P's products even though our own experts have decided in favor of Q. A Wall Street analyst blasts our Return On Investment, and we must give the impression of delivering new products faster.

Against such a deluge the manager must act as conduit, filter and umbrella. Conduit, to ensure that the most important and valuables demands from the outside world get properly addressed. Filter, to ensure that they reach the developers purified from any superfluous aspects. Umbrella, to deflect unwanted precipitation.

Instead what you sometimes see is non-technical managers who magnify the outside world's crises and, for good measure, add a few of their own making. This is not a very useful contribution. Managers should help weather the storms, not throw the windows open.

This part of the manager's role exists in all disciplines but particularly relevant in software. Programming — in the broad sense used in this book, encompassing analysis, design, implementation, maintenance and the other components of a seamless lifecycle — is a difficult intellectual activity which requires concentration and dedication. Programmers will not strive in an environment where they always have to deal with the crisis *du jour*. Technical managers know this and will respect the developers' desire to be shielded from the agitation of the moment. Non-technical managers may not fully appreciate the need for intellectual calm.

None of this means that managers, technical or not, should be in awe of the developers and never disturb them. Like everyone else, programmers can get complacent; they can forget the importance of deadlines, the constraints of product marketing, the needs of customers, the policies of the company, the order of priorities. The manager is entitled to intrude from time to time, take a close look, and question what all that concentration and busy airs have actually produced. And once in a while a real crisis will erupt. But the rest of the time it is the manager's duty to make sure that little tempests stay in their teacups.

WHAT THE NON-TECHNICAL MANAGER CAN DO

From all the preceding discussion one might get the impression that non-technical managers can only bring disaster to a project. But nothing could be further from the truth! Non-technical managers can be an invaluable resource if they understand their job. One can even argue that in some circumstances a non-technical manager might do better than a technically savvy manager.

Indeed what makes it really infuriating to see managers wasting their time in uncalled actions of the type discussed so far is that when they properly focus their energies they can bring considerable benefit to a software development team. One of the best things that can happen to a project is the availability of an outsider with management skills and enough good sense to know when to stay away and when to intervene.

The principal contribution that such a manager can make is to bring a healthy business perspective to the development. It is all too easy for technically-inclined people — programmers, but also managers with a technical background — to lose sight of the business issues: the customers, the market, the competition, the timing of deliveries, the relative importance of each product's various features. Here the non-technical manager can play several roles:

- *Resident skeptic*: What does this do for me? Is this feature really worth an extra two person-months? How many extra copies will it sell?

- *Customer advocate*: This new facility you are talking about sounds great, but what about all these calls from Cresus-Midas saying their system crashes every once in a while for no apparent reason?

- *On-site dumbbell*: Can you explain again what double-dispatch polymorphism is about? I know you tried last week but I am afraid I may have fallen asleep. Yet if I don't understand it our marketing people may have trouble selling it (you know they are not much smarter than I am).

What makes these roles so essential is the peculiar nature of software development and software developers. The character traits of good programmers, already noted in an earlier chapter, often include perfectionism. Most of the time (when applied to quality, for example), perfectionism is a positive trait, to be encouraged by the manager. But occasionally it may mean spending a considerable amount of time on an issue that looks important and challenging to a developer but is of minor business relevance. In such cases the contribution of a non-technical manager with good business sense can be essential to bring everyone back on earth.

THE DEBUGGER THAT WOULD HAVE COST AN ARM AND A LEG

To illustrate cases in which perfectionism can cause more harm than good here is a little example from ISE's own experience.

When we were developing our flagship environment, ISE Eiffel 3, the design of the debugging tools led to a multi-process architecture. The user application is in one process; the environment, including the debugger, is in another process.

> This use of two separate processes was necessary for several reasons. For example, if an exception occurs during the test execution of a software system under development, the environment must be able to catch the exception *before* it is passed on to the application; that way the environment will be able to provide the user with all its debugging and browsing facilities, so that the user can understand why the exception occurred, find the corresponding bug in the software, and correct it. If everything resided in a single process, the exception would terminate the session — not the kind of debugging aid that you would expect from a software development environment!

Once this architecture had been designed and a first version of the implementation produced, a developer remarked that since the application and the environment used different processes communicating through a standardized protocol (based on "sockets") they did not have to reside on the same machine, or for that matter on machines of compatible architectures; we had in fact all the necessary mechanisms in place to support remote debugging, where the application would be running (say) on a Sun in Tokyo and being debugged on-line from a PC running Windows in Santa Barbara. This looked like a really nifty idea and the originator of this idea, who had presented it as requiring a fairly straightforward extension of the basic scheme, was given the go-ahead to implement it.

Then as weeks went by this particular functionality started to take up a growing part of the development effort and to cause difficulties and extra work in more and more other components of the system — so much so that at some stage we had to sit down and ask the obvious question: is it really worth it? The answer was that the extra facility had not been part of the original specification; had not been announced to customers and prospects waiting for the new release; had not surfaced in any of the requests from the field. To put it simply, we had no guarantee that it would sell a single extra copy in the short term. Although potentially useful in the future, at the moment it was simply delaying the release and taking away our energy from the features that our customers badly wanted us to implement.

The conclusion was straightforward enough: we shelved that part of the development and concentrated on the pressing issues. Not that the idea of remote debugging was bad; it simply was not worth the consequences — for the time being.

The prudent slogan NRM applies to such cases: *Next Release, Maybe*.

COSTS AND BENEFITS

The Case of the Debugger That Would Have Cost an Arm and a Leg is a good example of where a manager with a strong business-oriented and customer-oriented perspective can make a difference. Technical managers can have this perspective too, of course, but they are never fully inoculated against the danger of falling in love with an idea just because of its technical elegance.

The problem is that sometimes technical attraction is a good initial reason to explore an idea. In particular, it would be wrong to react to the above example by commenting: "The remote debugging capability was not part of the original specification; it should never have been considered in the first place. The programmer who came up with this idea should have been sent back to his original assignment; then the problem would never have occurred. It is not a programmer's business to question the specification." If that was your reaction when reading the above example, I am afraid you may have been subjected to too much waterfall-like ideology ("Do the requirements at the beginning, then don't ever change them").

In the seamless approach to software construction fostered by object technology, we do expect the design and implementation to give us new ideas about the system's functionalities. It is not just that we are prepared for such possibilities: we consider them desirable. This is the idea of **reversibility**, studied in the discussion of the O-O lifecycle (see "REVERSIBILITY", page 49). The software process must be organized so as to enable the development to benefit from such late ideas for improvement.

A manager of the old school, who believes that analysis is only done by analysts and that implementers must only implement, will have little success in the world of object-oriented software development — and should not be surprised if the best programmers leave, one after the other, for organizations more attuned to the value of input from talented implementers and to the benefits of a seamless, reversible software construction process where design and implementation can influence specification, not just the other way around.

The question, then, is not whether we should accept unplanned developments, input from the developers, feedback from implementation to analysis, and programmer perfectionism. These phenomena are natural and in many cases beneficial. The task of the manager is to distinguish the beneficial cases from the others, by applying business criteria to evaluate the developers' technical suggestions and arguments.

This task is representative of the general role of the non-technical manager: bringing to the project the proper business perspective.

Appendix

O-O: the technology

The previous chapters have emphasized the managerial aspects of object technology. Chapter 2 presented the essential concepts, but stayed at a high level of generality. Here is a chance to take a more detailed look, focusing on the area where the approach makes it key contribution: software development methodology.

Since the discussion covers some of the material summarized and previewed in chapter 2, you should expect a few repetitions from that earlier presentation.

THE ARCHITECTURE

As noted in the earlier discussion, the object-oriented approach primarily affects the architecture of software systems, as defined by each system's organization into coherent pieces, or modules, and by how these modules interact with each other.

The starting point of object orientation is a general form of software architecture that is the reverse of the traditional one. Earlier methods told developers to decompose their systems into modules reflecting the system's **functions**. For example a mail-order system would be decomposed into parts corresponding to invoicing, shipping, billing and others. Each one of these parts would be further decomposed under the same lines, down to the level of functions that were simple enough to be implemented by small program modules known as subroutines, subprograms or (quite to the point) functions. Each subroutine would take care of a well-defined part of the job, for example

Process new order received through the toll-free number

This idea of function pervaded the entire structure of software systems, and the entire development process. Even at higher levels of abstraction, during the early phases of projects — "analysis" and "design" — the emphasis was on identifying steps of the process under study.

The object-oriented approach reverses this perspective. Instead of subroutines the method focuses on data abstractions, also called **classes**. The mail-order system, for example, might have such classes as *CUSTOMER*, *ORDER* and *SHIPMENT_RECORD*.

How do we use classes? At first they might seem like glorified data types. After all it is not a novelty to have a program include descriptions of such notions as customer order or shipment record. If you are familiar with common programming languages, you will remember that the "structures" of Cobol, C and PL/I and the "records" of Pascal provide such descriptions. But there is a big difference: in object-oriented development, classes do not just yield data descriptions; they also provide the backbone of our software architectures.

This is where an object-oriented solution will distinguish itself. The classes are not just data type descriptions scattered across the modules; they *are* the modules! The mail-order system will have modules corresponding to the classes listed earlier; an Electronic Funds Transfer (EFT) system may have modules such as *TRANSACTION, CURRENCY, RATE,* corresponding to the application's major data types. In either example there may also be more software-specific modules such as *LIST, DATABASE_LOCK* and *HASH_TABLE,* each of which corresponds to a data structure commonly used in programming: lists of elements of a similar type, for example a list of orders or currencies; temporary locks put on the database to avoid access conflicts; hash tables, that is to say dictionaries of elements each identified by a certain key.

This observation leads to a principle of object orientation:

> **OBJECT-ORIENTED STRUCTURING PRINCIPLE**
>
> A pure object-oriented approach makes no difference between the notions of module and type. Both are based on the concept of **class**, or data abstraction.

Every module is a type: it is based on a certain data abstraction such as *CURRENCY.* Every type is a module. The notion that unites the two traditional concepts, serving both as the only kind of module and as the only basis for types, is the class.

This notion — class — is, with its consequences, what defines the object-oriented approach.

INSTANCES AND OBJECTS

A class describes a certain general category, for example the abstract notion of order or currency. In that category, we may identify specific representatives, for example a specific engine, transaction, device or list. Such a representative is called an **instance** of the class. For example an instance of class *CURRENCY* is a particular currency, or more precisely its computer representation in the form of a data structure used in the EFT system.

An **object** is an instance of a class.

THE FATE OF FUNCTIONS

With the emphasis on types as a basis for modules we have only looked at one half of the software world: the data part. The object-oriented method focuses on this part to derive the module structure, using classes such as *ORDER, CURRENCY* or *LIST.* But what happens then to the other half — the functions? We saw that functions do not determine the architecture; but of course they must still be somewhere: without them our software would not do anything. We could have a database, perhaps, but not an executable software system.

The answer is simple. The functions are as important as ever, but they must defer to the data abstractions (the object types) when it comes to defining the architecture. In traditional, function-based decomposition, you would have found descriptions of data, in the form of type or structure declarations, as part of the descriptions of functions (the subroutines). Here it will be the reverse: any function will be part of a class. So each function is permitted to live, but only if it pleads allegiance to a data abstraction — a class. The terms of the treaty are rather unequal: the object types own the land, each one of them ruling over a module; the functions toil for the types.

The types that rule the local module chiefdoms are the classes. Their serfs, describing functions, may be called **features**. (You will also encounter the term *method*. "Feature" is slightly more general.)

Here is an example.

| *length* *font* | **WORD** | *set_font* *hyphenate_on* *hyphenate_off* |

| *word_count* *justified?* *space_before* *space_after* | **PARAGRAPH** | *add_word* *remove_word* *justify* *unjustify* *add_space_before* *add_space_after* |

| *height* *width* | **PAGE** | *print* *set_height* *set_width* |

QUERIES   COMMANDS

SOME EXAMPLE CLASSES AND THEIR FEATURES

This view could be extracted from the description of a system for document processing. Three classes are shown: *WORD*, *PARAGRAPH* and *PAGE*, each represented by an elliptic bubble (this is a common convention) and corresponding to the software representations of the corresponding notions. Of course in the actual system there will be far more classes; and many of them will correspond to data abstractions such as *LIST* which, rather than being directly related to tangible notions such as paragraph, are pure software notions.

Next to each class bubble some of the features of the class have been shown. For example, the features of class *WORD*, representing operations applicable to any instance of the class — any object representing a word — include:

• *length*: indicate the length of the word (the number of characters).

• *font*: indicate the current font for the word.

• *set_font*: change the font to a specified one.

• *hyphenate_on, hyphenate_off*: turn hyphenation on or off for this word.

The other two classes shown have features with similarly self-explanatory names.

The features are of two kinds: **queries** and **commands**. The queries, appearing on the left of the figure, return information on the properties of an object at a certain instant of the software's execution: the length of a word, whether a paragraph is justified, the width of a page. The features on the right — the commands — can change the object: assign a new font to a word, add a word to a paragraph, print a page.

FUNCTIONS IN THE TRADITIONAL VIEW

Although the concepts introduced so far are elementary, they already represent a revolutionary departure from traditional views of software. One of the most significant innovation is that the method puts commands and queries on an equal footing. Even people who have used an object-oriented language for a while (without necessarily having received the corresponding training in the method) sometimes still have trouble grasping this idea. To understand what it means, consider how a more traditional approach would handle a notion such as *PARAGRAPH* in a text-processing system. At the implementation level (that is to say, in the program itself) you would have a "type declaration" looking something like this:

```
                    -- Warning: this is not an object-oriented software extract!
type PARAGRAPH is
    record
            word_count: INTEGER;
            justified: BOOLEAN;
            ... Other fields ...
    end
```

This is a description of a type of data structures to be created at execution time, each with a field that contains an integer value *word_count* representing the paragraph's number of words, another field containing a boolean value *justified* saying whether the paragraph is to be justified or not, and possibly other fields.

Where the program needs to manipulate paragraphs it will use variables declared of the corresponding type, for example

```
last_paragraph: PARAGRAPH
```

representing a data structure which, at some point during execution, might look like this:

last_paragraph
(instance of class *PARAGRAPH*)

word_count	12
justified	*false*
Other fields	

A DATA STRUCTURE IN TRADITIONAL PROGRAMMING

Then there will be operations to manipulate such objects. For example the program may include a subroutine *add_word* such that a call to that subroutine, written

add_word (*last_paragraph*, *user_input*, *8*)

changes the internal data structure to reflect the addition of a new word, given by the variable *user_input*, after the eighth word in the paragraph represented by the above object.

Other operations, typically implemented as subroutines, would make it possible to remove a word (*remove_word*), set the paragraph to justified mode (*justify*), set it to unjustified mode (*unjustify*).

In this traditional approach, no one would ever think of considering the fields of the *PARAGRAPH* objects (*word_count*, *justified*) as similar in nature to the operations (*add_word* and so on). The fields are part of the data description; the operations are part of the program — the set of algorithms defined by the software.

This example has been discussed at the implementation level. But the practice of considering descriptions of the data and of the processing as completely separate pervades traditional views of software at all levels. Traditional database description techniques, for example, are purely data-oriented; it has in fact been a central tenet of the database world, until the advent of object-oriented databases, that one should store, describe and manage data in a form that is not influenced by its usage. (This is sometimes described by the catchphrase *program-data independence*.) In a different area, common methods for analysis and design, such as entity-relationship modeling and Structured Analysis, also consider the data and the processing as belonging to different parts of the world. For example the Data Flow Diagrams (DFD) which constitute the basis of the Structured Analysis method put the data in nodes of the graph and the processing in edges:

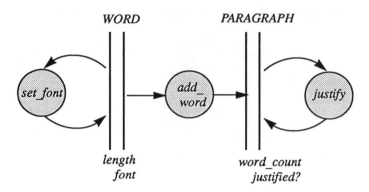

A DATA FLOW DIAGRAM
(*WARNING*: this is *not* an object-oriented diagram! See text.)

AN UNEQUAL TREATY

In the pre-O-O view, as shown by the preceding examples, we had data structures such as words and paragraphs — which could be called objects just as legitimately as in the "object-oriented" approach, showing once again the dangers of this terminology — and we had operations (processing) such as *set_font* and *add_word* that act on these data.

With object-oriented development, whatever the level — O-O analysis, O-O design, O-O implementation — the view changes radically. The concept of an operation as a stand-alone element, separate from the objects, disappears. Instead, every operation is attached to an object. As a result we make no fundamental distinction between a feature such as *word_count*, which classically would have been viewed as describing object fields, and one such as *add_word*, which would have been viewed as a piece of the algorithm. We see both as features applicable to paragraph objects (instances of the class *PARAGRAPH*).

These observations lead to the rule that summarizes the object-oriented form of software architecture by defining the (undemocratic) social relations between masters and serfs in the object-oriented software world:

> ## THE OBJECT ORIENTATION TREATY
>
> In a pure object-oriented approach, every operation belongs to exactly one class.

The Object Orientation Treaty is the starting point for object-oriented architectures, all organized around data types, to which operations are attached. The aim is the one defined at the beginning of this chapter: yielding more flexible software architectures that will support extendibility and reusability.

This discussion, of course, has not *proved* that the O-O form of modularization makes it possible to achieve these aims; this is the aim of more in-depth presentations of the method, and the argument is in particular made in detail in the book *Object-Oriented Software Construction* (see the bibliography of chapter 2). As we go along, we will encounter a number of informal reasons to support the Object Orientation Treaty.

RELATIONS BETWEEN CLASSES

To build a software architecture, we need to make two kinds of decision: selecting the modules; and defining their interconnections. We have the general answer to the first issue: use the data types.

The answer to the second problem, connections, will also be essential for ensuring extendibility, reusability and reliability. Each of these goals requires that we restrict the amount of communication that may occur between modules, that is to say, the degree to which a module may depend on others:

- For extendibility, any dependency means that a change to a module may require changes to the modules on which it depends — and then to those on which *they* depend, and so on.

- For reusability, dependencies mean that we cannot reuse a module without also having access to all the other modules on which it depends directly or indirectly.

- For reliability, dependencies mean potential inconsistencies and interface problems, a major source of hard-to-find bugs.

Traditional software construction techniques have failed to limit dependencies. The result, as already noted, is intricate architectures where a module may depend on many others, as in a castle of cards where removing any piece will cause the entire edifice to collapse. This is the primary reason for the lack of extendibility of much of today's software: changes requested by customers are much more difficult to carry out than they should be. The famous "application backlog" of the MIS industry is largely a consequence of this situation: if developers spend all their time painstakingly making changes to existing applications, they have no time for new ones.

One of the worst causes of dependency, fostered by many programming languages (including unfortunately some that claim to be object-oriented) is the *global variable* mechanism, allowing a module to declare a variable that many other modules, or even all modules, will be able to access and change. This facility introduces tight coupling between modules — since those which access the variable become dependent on those which can change it — and squelches any hope for decentralized software architectures.

The object-oriented method follows a much stricter approach. When applied properly, it only leaves room for two kinds of inter-module relation: **client** and **heir** (the latter also known as inheritance).

It is convenient to represent the client relation, in graphical sketches of a system's structure, by a double arrow going from a class to one of which it is a client — known as a *supplier* of the first:

A CLIENT-SUPPLIER RELATIONSHIP

A class is a client of another if it relies on its features for the needs of its own features. For example the class *PARAGRAPH* will be a client of class *WORD* since the features of class *PARAGRAPH* will manipulate words — through the features of *WORD*.

Like client-supplier relations between businesses, communication between client and supplier classes will benefit from precise specifications of their mutual obligations. This is the concept of *Design by Contract*, reviewed later in this chapter.

The client-supplier relation between two classes also implies, in most cases, an execution-time relation between the corresponding objects — the instances of these classes. Here, for example, a paragraph will consist, among other components, of a list of words; so each paragraph object will contain references to some words:

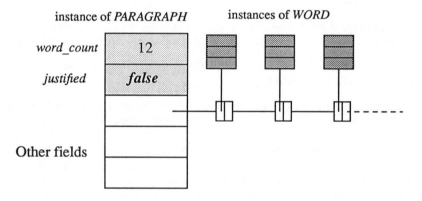

A PARAGRAPH THAT "HAS" WORDS

Another way of expressing this observation is to note that if we look at instances rather than classes, the client relation is the **has** relation: here every paragraph object "has" one or more word objects. ("Paragraph object" means instance of class *PARAGRAPH*, and so on.) The reverse of that relation is sometimes called **part-of**; for example a word may be a part of a paragraph. But the supplier relation is more general than "part-of".

The second relation, inheritance, addresses a different need. In many applications one may need classes describing common neighboring concepts. For example our text processing system may consider that a document is a sequence of "chunks", where each chunk is a paragraph or some other element such as a figure. (Examples of consecutive chunks in a text are, in the document that you are now reading, the present paragraph, the previous one, and the figure preceding them.) Class *CHUNK* and class *PARAGRAPH* will have a number of features in common, for example:

• *space_before*, *space_after* (queries).

• *add_space_before*, *add_space_after* (commands).

But *CHUNK* is the more general notion, and *PARAGRAPH* the more specific, meaning that it has more features; for example *justify* only makes sense for a paragraph, but not necessarily for a chunk (the chunk might be a figure, which is not subject to justification.)

The object-oriented method, with its emphasis on reusability, naturally seeks to take advantage of this commonality. It would be a pity to duplicate the shared functionality. We will describe class *PARAGRAPH* as an **heir** of class *CHUNK*. The graphical convention uses a single arrow:

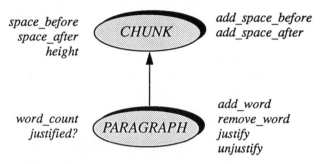

A CLASS AND ONE OF ITS HEIRS

The heir link means that *PARAGRAPH* retains — "inherits" — the features of *CHUNK*, to which it may of course add its own. Not shown are other classes, such as *FIGURE*, that may also be heirs of *CHUNK*; they will appear later in this chapter.

Inheritance has more properties, which will be seen shortly. For the moment it is sufficient to consider its role in defining inter-module communication. If client was "has", inheritance is "is"; for example the above example states that every paragraph (every instance of class *PARAGRAPH*) is also an instance of class *CHUNK*.

Together, the two relations provide enough power to cover all possible forms of inter-module communication:

> **OBJECT-ORIENTED COMMUNICATION PRINCIPLE**
>
> In a pure object-oriented approach, only two relations are permitted between classes: client and heir.

This insistence on "permitting" only certain relations may appear authoritarian. But that is not the point. The key to software reusability and extendibility — and a factor in ensuring many other software qualities — is to enable the construction of modular, flexible software architectures. As with information hiding (see "INFORMATION HIDING AND THE MANAGER", page 14, and next), restricting the amount of inter-module communication is not a matter of restricting the freedom of software developers; it is a matter of *enabling* them to build and maintain large systems. This requires remaining in control of their potential complexity, and there is no other solution than placing stringent controls on the chief source of complexity: inter-module communication.

For the leader of any software project using object-oriented ideas — and expecting them to yield the advertized benefits — one of the primary responsibilities is to enforce these controls, beginning with the selection of an object-oriented language that makes such enforcement possible.

INFORMATION HIDING

Describing classes in terms of their features is another departure from the traditional approaches to similar issues.

In those approaches a record or structure declaration would describe the physical makeup of objects of a certain type. For example, to describe the implementation of paragraphs illustrated by an earlier figure reproduced here:

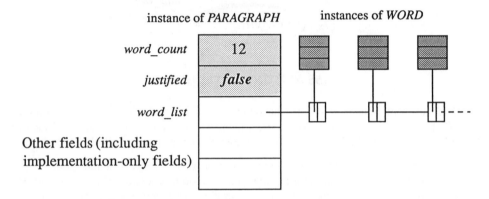

A PARAGRAPH OBJECT

you could use a declaration (also shown earlier) describing any *PARAGRAPH* object as consisting of the fields that appear on the figure:

```
              -- Warning: this is again not an object-oriented software extract!
type PARAGRAPH is
    record
        word_count: INTEGER;
        justified: BOOLEAN;
        word_list: LIST_OF_WORDS;
        ... Other fields ...
    end
```

If you are in charge of writing or maintaining the part of the system that is responsible for that description, this is the information that you need. But not if you are using the notion of *PARAGRAPH* for the needs of another module! Then the internal structure of *PARAGRAPH* objects is irrelevant to your needs. Along with useful features such as *word_count* that structure may contain many fields that only address implementation needs and should not be used by client modules.

The object-oriented method avoids this problem by defining an object type, as represented by a class, not in terms of internal representation but in terms of available operations — the features of the class. For example a *PARAGRAPH* object is not known to clients of this class through its implementation; it is instead defined by the applicable operations — the features of a class. A paragraph is an object to which you can apply the commands *add_word*, *remove_word*, *justify* and *unjustify*, and the queries *word_count* and *justified*. Internally it may have many other properties; but the clients of class *PARAGRAPH* will only be able to use those which the author of class *PARAGRAPH* has deemed fit for external consumption:

> ### INFORMATION HIDING PRINCIPLE
>
> A principal duty of the designer of any class is to define precisely which ones of the features of the class will be accessible to its clients, and which ones they will not be permitted to use.
>
> A principal duty of an object-oriented language (whether meant for analysis, design or implementation) is to enforce these decisions by ensuring that a client class cannot access a feature unless the supplier class has made it available to it.

To apply this principle, the designer of every class will assign an **export status** to every feature of the class: the feature is either *exported* or *secret*. Other terms are also used: *public* in the first case; *private* or *hidden* in the second. In addition it is possible to make a feature *selectively available* to certain clients only.

In the example you may have noted that an exported query such as *word_count* may directly correspond to a field of *PARAGRAPH* objects in the traditional, no-information-hiding solution. But the differences are considerable:

- In the traditional approach any client that has access to *PARAGRAPH* and hence to *word_count* will also be able to modify the *word_count* field of any *PARAGRAPH* object. With object-oriented information hiding this is not the case any more: the designer of class *PARAGRAPH* may export feature *word_count* in "read-only" mode, so that clients can access the corresponding values but not modify them. To make *word_count* modifiable by clients you have to write a small command *set_word_count* and export that command. The same technique was assumed above in the case of the *justified* query, whose value can be changed through two exported commands *justify* and *unjustify*. It gives class designers the needed flexibility for defining the appropriate privileges granted to various clients for each feature.

- Although *word_count* is an exported feature, it does not necessarily correspond to a field in the representation of each *PARAGRAPH* object as pictured above. Instead of the representation shown there you could for example, if space were tight, dispense with the corresponding field, while still offering a *word_count* feature in the class: when a client requests the value of that feature you simply compute it by traversing the list of words (accessing through the field marked *word_list*) and counting the number of items in the list. In this case feature *word_count* is computed, rather than stored; but to client classes this makes no difference, except possibly for the time it takes to obtain the result of the feature during execution.

• You can change from one representation to the other without causing any change in the client classes, which will continue to use the *word_count* feature without having to rely on knowledge of how it is actually implemented.

This ability to implement a feature by either computation (time) or storage (space) without affecting the client's way of accessing the feature, and in fact without having to tell the authors of client classes of the change, is one of the important consequences of information hiding.

ASSERTIONS AND DESIGN BY CONTRACT

To make information hiding practical, and to enable reuse of classes, object technology requires systematic techniques for documentation. Assertions help solve this problem; they will also play a key role in addressing the reliability goal.

Assertions are elements of specification integrated with the software. Traditionally, software has been viewed as an operational product — a sequence of instructions for the computer to execute. In reality software texts have a much broader role; they are read not only by computing machinery but also by humans. With assertions, you can let the software describe what it is trying to do, not just how it goes about doing it. This also advances the goal of seamlessness: many of the assertions will be produced at the analysis stage, or at the design stage, and will remain in the final product that they will help to build.

Here is a simple example. Class *PARAGRAPH*, as noted, may have a command *add_ space_after* that inserts vertical space, measured in number of lines, after a paragraph:

> *add_space_after* (*lines*: *REAL*)
> 　　　　-- Add *lines* lines after the current paragraph
>
> 　　...

This procedure is actually inherited from *CHUNK*, but let us assume for a while that everything is done in *PARAGRAPH*. The number of lines is declared as a *REAL*, so that a fractional number will be acceptable. A typical call in a client might be

> *first_paragraph.add_space_after* (*3.5*)

which causes the feature *add_space_after*, with argument *3.5*, to be called on the *PARAGRAPH* object that *first_paragraph* will denote at run time. The result is to add a vertical space, 3.5 lines high, after the *first_paragraph*. (Such feature calls, which make the bulk of the execution of an object-oriented system, are also known as **message passing**: we may view the above as sending to the object a "message" asking it to add the space.)

The line in the above feature declaration beginning with -- is known as a header comment. It gives some documentation about what the feature does, but that documentation is rather informal. With assertions we can be more precise. Here is what we can write:

add_space_after (*lines*: *REAL*)
        -- Add *lines* lines after the current paragraph.
    require
        height > 0;
        lines >= 0
    ensure
        *height = **old** height + lines*

This version has two assertions: a precondition, introduced by **require**, and a postcondition, introduced by **ensure**. The precondition states what initial conditions a client should satisfy to be entitled to call the feature; the postcondition states what will be true on return. Here we are saying that:

- One may add space after a paragraph only if it is non-empty (that is to say, with non-zero height) and if the number of lines of the requested space is non-negative. (The first of these requirements may be too strong, but let us just assume that it is what the author of class *PARAGRAPH* has decided.)

- After a call to *add_space_after*, the paragraph's height will have been increased by *lines*, the value of the argument (such as *3.5* in the above example call). The notation *old height* refers to the value of *height* on entry to the feature.

Executing the feature may do quite a few things besides increasing the value of *height*. But the postcondition captures one of the essential effects by stating the relationship between the old and new values of *height*, both observable by the client.

Such a precondition-postcondition pair illustrates the use of assertions to express the terms of the **contract** that the author of the class offers to the clients. Here the assertions define the contract for feature *add_space_after*:

add_space_ after	**OBLIGATIONS**	**BENEFITS**
Client	(*Satisfy precondition:*) Ensure paragraph is non-empty, and requested spacing is non-negative.	(*From postcondition:*) Get requested spacing after paragraph.
Supplier	(*Satisfy postcondition:*) Update text to insert requested spacing after paragraph.	(*From precondition:*) Simpler processing thanks to the assumption that paragraph is non-empty and requested spacing is non-negative.

Like any contract between people or between companies, this contract describes the benefits expected by both parties, and the obligations that each has to meet in order to obtain the benefits. Benefits for one correspond to obligations for the other.

Design by Contract is a powerful metaphor for software construction. It leads developers and managers to view the construction of a software system as consisting of a large number of contract decisions, large and small, between modules cooperating towards a common goal.

Most of the time, reliability problems — bugs — are interface problems. They result from an inconsistency between two modules, one of them expecting something and the other doing something slightly different. These interface problems are the nightmare of software developers, because the inconsistencies are often small (such as the typical "off by one" errors that show up in borderline cases) and manifest themselves in rare cases only. Often they do not occur in testing but suddenly appear in full-scale production runs.

The first contribution of object technology towards a solution to this central problem of software development has been highlighted above: by enforcing information hiding and outlawing global variables, the method puts drastic limits on inter-module communication. But this is only a first step, since communication, however limited, will still occur. Design by Contract provides the required second component of the solution by encouraging software developers to base the remaining inter-module interactions on precise definitions of mutual expectations and promises. Each client module states what it needs; each supplier module states what it guarantees; the task of the software developer is to check that the guarantee is at least as much as the need.

This conception of a software system as a myriad of client-supplier relations, based on an abstract but precise description of each party's contribution, lies at the heart of the object-oriented approach to the construction of reliable software. Both abstraction and precision are essential: *precision* because if we are interested in bug-free systems we cannot accept hazy details; *abstraction* because the only way to handle complexity is to force modules and their designers to interact solely on the basis of each other's essential, externally meaningful properties, leaving in peace the internal details that are not significant to the outside.

APPLICATIONS OF ASSERTIONS

Assertions have a number of practical uses in the object-oriented method.

In the spirit of Design by Contract, they are a powerful aid to the construction of O-O systems at all stages, beginning with analysis. You can model the properties of a future system through classes and features equipped with assertions; this makes it possible to be precise without over-specifying, resolving the dilemma of traditional analysis methods that err between the Charybdis of imprecision (typified by he bubbles and arrows of Structured Analysis) and the Scylla of over-specification (which always tempts the analyst, in the pursuit of precision, to write an implementation-oriented description — losing abstraction and committing too early).

Another important application of assertions is documentation. In the final version of a class there will be many implementation details; for example our above example feature may appear as

add_space_after (*lines*: *REAL*) *is*

>   -- Add *lines* lines after the current paragraph

>   *require*

>>   *height > 0*;

>>   *lines >= 0*

>   *do*

>>   ... Instructions implementing the feature's specification ...

>   *ensure*

>>   *height = old height + lines*

where the "... Instructions ..." part can be long and detailed. To provide a class documentation, you need to state what the features do, but not how they do it, which would be too low-level for the needs of client authors (that is to say, developers writing classes that may need to rely on this class). The **short form** of a class addresses this need: it discards the implementation-related aspects, in particular the *do* clauses, but keeps the client-relevant parts and in particular the assertions. It expresses the set of contracts defined by the class.

The short form can serve as the basic form of documentation for object-oriented software. A system's documentation is viewed here not as a product to be written and maintained on its own, but as a component of the software, which can be extracted from it by automatic tools. This makes it easier to ensure that the software and its documentation, as they both evolve, remain consistent (if there is anything worse than no documentation, it certainly is *wrong* documentation).

Yet another application of assertions is testing, debugging and, more generally, quality assurance. Traditional approaches to testing and debugging lack a precise definition of what you are looking for. With assertions, you can associate with every feature, and more generally with each class, a specification of the intended effect — the contract. Bugs, then, are cases in which the implementation deviates from the contract. A compiler for an object-oriented language that supports assertions will be able, on option, to generate code that checks assertions at run time, and triggers a run-time signal (an *exception*) if an assertion is found to be violated.

This is one of the most effective techniques I know to find and correct bugs — at least those bugs which still remain when static typing (see later in this Appendix) and Design by Contract have been applied from the beginning.

> Whether you are a manager or a developer, is difficult, until you have practiced this technique, to realize the benefits it can bring to reliability. It can actually change your entire outlook on software development.

INVARIANTS

This treatment of assertions has by nature been cursory. Further discussions may be found in bibliographical references given at the end of chapters 2 and 6. But one more point needs to be mentioned briefly. Along with preconditions and postconditions, an important use of assertions is for *class invariants*.

In contrast with the other two kinds, an invariant does not characterize an individual feature but the class as a whole. It describes integrity constraints that must be satisfied by all instances of the class whenever they are accessible by clients. For example a simple invariant clause for a class *LINE* in our hypothetical text-processing system might state

> *invariant*
> > *character_count >= 0*;
> > *space_count >= 0*;
> > *length >= 0*;
> > *enclosing_paragraph.justified* **implies** (*letter_count + space_count = length*)

where the last line states that if the enclosing paragraph is justified, the sum of the number of non-blank characters (*character_count*) and the number of spaces is equal to the length of the line. (*a* **implies** *b* is a logical implication, false if and only if *a* is true and *b* is false.) An invariant property must be maintained by every feature that acts on the corresponding instances.

It is one of the great achievements of object-oriented software construction to have given us the tools for expressing such constraints, which in traditional methods often remain unspoken, and then to use them to document, test and debug the systems that we build with them, so as to achieve a much higher degree of reliability than was previously possible.

GENERICITY AND INHERITANCE

The basic notion of class seen so far can be made more general in two ways.

First, any software that deals with collections of objects will need class-parameterized classes, also known as generic classes. The idea is that if you want to manipulate such structures as a list of paragraphs, a list of chapters or a list of words you will not want to write three different classes — *LIST_OF_PARAGRAPHS* and so on. Such classes would be almost identical: they would all have features such as *count* to give the number of items in a list, *put* to insert an item into the list and the like. All that would differ would be the types of the entities being manipulated. For example *LIST_OF_PARAGRAPHS* would have the feature

> *first*: *PARAGRAPH* **is**
> > -- The first item in the list
> *require*
> > *not empty*
> *do*
> > ...
> *end*

The corresponding feature in classes *LIST_OF_CHAPTERS* and *LIST_OF_WORDS* would only differ by having *first* declared of type *CHAPTER* and *WORD*.

Such quasi-duplication would clearly be incompatible with the goal of software reusability. Yet it is not satisfactory to declare simply a *LIST* class; we must maintain the type consistency of our software, and be able to guarantee, for example, that a list of words does not contain chapters, and a list of chapters does not contain words.

The solution is to parameterize. Genericity allows you to declare a class such as

class *LIST* [*G*] ***feature***
    first: *G* **is**
                -- The first item in the list
      require
          not *empty*
      do
          ...
      end;
    put (*x*: *G*; *i*: *INTEGER*) **is**
                -- Insert item *x* at position *i*
    ...

    ... Other features ...
end

This class represents a pattern which you can use by providing actual types (called **actual generic parameters**) for *G*. For example a client class can use the declaration

   my_book: *LIST* [*CHAPTER*]

using *CHAPTER* as the actual generic parameter. Within the class text, *G*, known as the **formal generic parameter**, serves as a placeholder for arbitrary types to be used as actual generic parameters. Note how the result of *first* and the first argument of *put* are declared of type *G*; this means these features will use objects of type *CHAPTER* when applied to a list object of type *LIST* [*CHAPTER*] such as *my_book*, objects of type *PARAGRAPH* when applied to a *LIST* [*PARAGRAPH*] and so on.

This form of genericity provides us with much needed flexibility without forcing us to renounce the benefits of a typed approach, where every entity in the software has a well-defined type which can be checked by various automatic mechanisms — not just compilers at implementation time, but also CASE tools at analysis time. (More on typing later.)

The other basic extension mechanism, complementing genericity, has already been previewed: inheritance. This facility allows you to specialize and generalize classes. For example, a generalization of *PARAGRAPH*, as seen above, is *CHUNK*; this class has specializations *PARAGRAPH* and *FIGURE*. *PARAGRAPH* itself may have the specialization *DISPLAY*, representing display paragraphs such as program extracts, for example in the present text the display that appears above on this page for class *LIST*. Here is the resulting part of the inheritance structure:

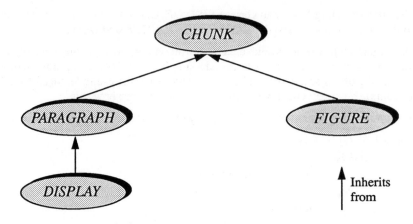

AN INHERITANCE STRUCTURE

Inheritance is the application to software construction of a central idea of science: classification. Scientists classify their domains of study to comprehend them: zoologists have taxonomies (classification systems) for animals, botanists for plants, mathematicians for the logical artefacts of the mind. In software we similarly need taxonomies to organize our data abstractions. This is the role of inheritance.

A taxonomy of the principal structures of computing science, covering basic data structures and common algorithms, has been proposed in the book *Reusable Software...* (see the reference on page 130).

INHERITANCE TECHNIQUES

Four techniques enable inheritance to exert an even deeper effect on the software process than the preceding introduction suggests. The techniques — redeclaration, polymorphism, dynamic binding and deferred classes — are individually important, but it is their combination that gives them their full meaning. Let us look at the first three; the last, which is particularly relevant to object-oriented analysis and design, will be explored in a later section (page 178).

A bit of terminology: a class that inherits from another is its *heir*, the other is the heir's *parent*. The *ancestors* of a class include the class itself, its parents, its grandparents and so on; the reverse notion is *descendant*.

Redeclaration makes it possible to be selective in what you inherit from a parent. If you want to change some of its features, you can redeclare them. For example the feature *add_space_after* may have different properties for a general paragraph and a display paragraph. If so, class *DISPLAY* will redeclare it, as represented graphically by the ++ mark:

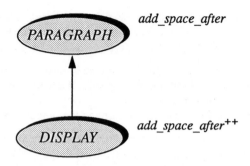

add_space_after

add_space_after^{++}

REDECLARING A FEATURE

Redeclaration gives us much needed flexibility in reuse. As noted at the beginning of chapter 2 (page 8), any reasonable approach to software construction will let you reuse a software element exactly as it is. The reality of software development is usually more demanding: it requires that you be able to combine reuse with adaptation — keep what you like from a software element, here a class, and change what is not adapted to the new context. All this should be done without affecting the original module and its existing clients. Redeclaration achieves this: the original class, here *PARAGRAPH*, is left untouched; class *DISPLAY* keeps what it likes from it — most of the features — and changes what has to be different.

Polymorphism is the ability to have a single entity of the software text denote run-time objects of more than one type. It is best illustrated by the case of generic structures. Assume that we have declared a list of the form

your_list: *LIST* [*CHUNK*]

then in the corresponding run-time structure it is possible to insert list elements containing instances of any of the descendant classes of *CHUNK*: *FIGURE*, *PARAGRAPH* and *DISPLAY*. At some point during execution the list might look like this:

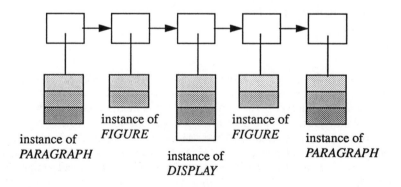

instance of
PARAGRAPH

instance of
FIGURE

instance of
DISPLAY

instance of
FIGURE

instance of
PARAGRAPH

A POLYMORPHIC LIST

The successive list items are of different types, although these types are all descendants of *CHUNK* in conformity with the above declaration of *your_list*. Such a data structure containing objects of different types is said to be polymorphic.

Dynamic binding is the requirement that follows naturally from the introduction of redeclaration and dynamic binding: making sure, if a feature that has several redeclarations and a call applies it to an object that is only known by a name of a higher-level type, that the call will trigger the version corresponding to the object's exact type.

Assume for example that you need to perform a traversal of *your_list*, using feature *item* to denote the element reached at an arbitrary stage of that traversal. Then *item* is only known as being of type *CHUNK*, although polymorphism implies that at run time it can denote an object of an arbitrary descendant type. If you execute a call of the form

   item.add_space_after (*3.5*)

you will want to make sure that instead of using a fixed feature each call automatically selects the appropriate version of *add_space_after*: the *PARAGRAPH* version for the first element in the example list of the above figure, the *FIGURE* version for the second, and so on.

Dynamic binding ensures this desired run-time behavior. It enables you to take a polymorphic data structure and apply a feature to its every one of its elements with the guarantee that every call will automatically adapt to the type of the corresponding element. For example you may process a list of prospects using a feature call of the form *prospect_ list.process*, where the feature *process* of the corresponding class executes a loop of the form

[O-O SCHEME]
   from
      start
   until
      after
   loop
      item.marketing_action
      forth
   end

The initialization gets you at the beginning of the list (*start*); the loop will proceed until you have moved past the end, as represented by *after*, and at each stage will advance to the next item through *forth*. The current element is *item*, to which each iteration applies *marketing_action*. Now assume that there are various kinds of prospect — "hot" new prospects, former customers that we hope to bring back to the fold, leads from shows and so on. We want to generate a different marketing action (personalized letter, telemarketing call, visit, special offer...) for each category. This will be achieved simply by having a different redeclaration of feature *marketing_action* for each of the corresponding classes (*LEAD_FROM_SHOW* and the like), each of which is a descendant of a general class *PROSPECT*. Dynamic binding takes care of the rest.

Using more traditional techniques it would of course have been possible to achieve a superficially similar goal using elaborate decision structures:

[NON-O-O SCHEME]

> *if show_sales_lead then*
>> ... Marketing action for show sales leads ...
>
> *elseif former_customer then*
>> ... Marketing action for former customers ...
>
> *elseif*
>
>> ...

Apart from being much simpler, the O-O solution based on classes, inheritance, redeclaration, polymorphism and dynamic binding has a major software engineering advantage: it lends itself to smooth evolution and reuse. If you want to extend your software to handle a new kind of prospect that you had not thought about before, all you need to do in the "O-O SCHEME" is to add a new class to the inheritance hierarchy to cover that new variant, and redeclare feature *marketing_action* accordingly. This takes care of the problem for any structure of the preceding form, relying on dynamic binding; if the technique has been applied thoroughly no existing software will need to be changed. But in the "NON-O-O-SCHEME" you would have to add an *elseif* branch to the text of *every* client that was using the notion of prospect! This phenomenon is one of the major sources of instability in traditional software engineering, and is responsible for many of the chain reactions of changes noted in earlier discussions.

What the combination of inheritance-based techniques brings here is the ability to take abstraction and information hiding to their extreme, by making each module as independent from the others as possible. The basic techniques of information hiding allowed a client to use a call such as *item.marketing_action* without knowing the details of the prospect object represented by *item*; but here we are going further: when several versions of *marketing_action* are available, we can defer the choice of version to use in this call until the very last moment that conceptually makes sense — each execution of the feature at run time.

Polymorphism, dynamic binding and the associated ideas are sometimes misunderstood as implementation tricks. To the contrary, they are architectural techniques, essential to the flexible, decentralized architectures of object-oriented software construction and its support for reusability and extendibility.

MULTIPLE INHERITANCE

It is often necessary, when using O-O techniques to model and implement systems, to use classifications that are based on more than one criterion. Multiple inheritance — the ability for a class to have two or more parents — addresses this need.

For example we might have developed a class *AIRPLANE* representing planes and, in a different part of our software, a class *ASSET* representing company assets. The features of *AIRPLANE* may include queries such as *passenger_capacity* as well as commands such as *fly_to*; the features of *ASSET* may include queries *purchase_value*, *depreciation* and *resale_value*, as well as commands *depreciate* and *resell*.

What if we need to cover the notion of company plane? Multiple inheritance provides the solution:

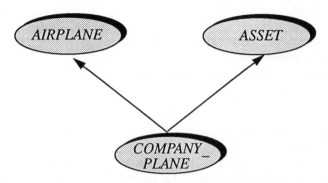

A CASE OF MULTIPLE INHERITANCE

Not having multiple inheritance would defeat reusability here: we would have to renounce one of the inheritance links and choose between the two parents (the other's features being duplicated). This is not acceptable.

Multiple inheritance raises a few technical problems, such as how to disambiguate name clashes between features inherited from different parents; good O-O language design will solve these problems in a straightforward way.

TYPING

One more important notion, arising from the reliability concern, has its place in this review of the principal O-O concepts: static typing.

The problem is easy to summarize. In the object-oriented approach the execution of software systems boils down to feature calls — "message passing" — of the form $x.f$ for some feature f, meaning: call f (possibly with arguments) on whatever object is attached to x at the time of the call. Dynamic binding guarantees that if more than one version of f is available the call will use the right one (the one that is appropriate for the type of that object); but static typing addresses an even more fundamental question: how do we know that there will always be at least one f?

Many examples of such a call have been seen above. Here is another. Assume a call of the form

   your_aircraft.lower_landing_gear

where *your_aircraft* denotes some flying object. Dynamic binding gives you a guarantee, if *your_aircraft* is polymorphic, that each call will trigger the proper version. For example, in the situation shown on the following figure, the version of *lower_landing_gear* for *BOEING_747_400* is not the same one as for *BOEING_747*, and if *your_aircraft* denotes an object of the more specialized type you will want the 400 version to be applied, even if *your_aircraft* is declared of type *BOEING_747* or something even more general such as *PLANE*.

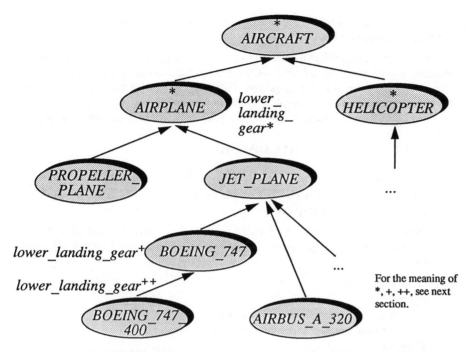

AN INHERITANCE STRUCTURE WITH REDECLARATIONS

For the sake of this discussion let us assume that only planes have landing gears, not helicopters, so that feature *lower_landing_gear* only appears at the level of class *AIRPLANE*, not *AIRCRAFT*. The statically typed approach to O-O development, used in Eiffel and assumed in the earlier examples, assumes that *your_aircraft* has been declared somewhere in the text, for example with one of the following two declarations:

> *your_aircraft*: *AIRCRAFT*   -- VERSION 1
> *your_aircraft*: *AIRPLANE*   -- VERSION 2

With version 2, the call *your_aircraft.lower_landing_gear* is safe: class *AIRPLANE* has a feature *lower_landing_gear*, ensuring that the call is always meaningful — even though every descendant may redeclare the feature as it pleases, so that dynamic binding may trigger several possible variants. But with version 1 there is no guarantee that the call will make sense: because of polymorphism, *your_aircraft* could in some execution be attached to an object of type *HELICOPTER*, to which *lower_landing_gear* is not applicable.

Static typing means that we require every entity x to be declared of some type C, and that the compiler or other tool checks that for any call $x.f$ the class corresponding to C contain a feature f. If that condition is not satisfied, the system containing the call will be rejected. This is a pessimistic policy, as evidenced by the above example: after all, this could be your lucky day at the flight control center, when all run-time values of *your_aircraft* will denote objects of type *BOEING_747* or *AIRBUS_A_320*. Static typing may indeed reject software that **might** work in some cases, because the aim is to guarantee that the software **will** work in all cases.

The other approach, typified by Smalltalk, is dynamic typing, which does not require type declarations such as the above, and waits until run time to find out whether a call will work, terminating abnormally if it does not. This may be acceptable for environments meant for experimentation or "prototyping", but not for production software. After all, run time is in most cases a bit late to find out whether your aircraft can lower its landing gear.

DEFERRED FEATURES AND CLASSES

The asterisk that marked feature *lower_landing_gear* of class *AIRPLANE* as well as that class itself, *AIRCRAFT* and *HELICOPTER* on the figure of page 177 is an indication that this feature and these classes are **deferred**.

A deferred feature is not implemented, although it may be specified through assertions. For example the feature *lower_landing_gear* could appear in class *AIRPLANE* under the general form

> *lower_landing_gear is*
>> *require*
>>> *altitude* >= *minimum_for_landing*;
>>> *altitude* <= *maximum_for_landing*
>> *deferred*
>> *ensure*
>>> *landing_gear.down*
>> *end*

The *deferred* indication, replacing the part where the non-deferred features of earlier examples had a list of instructions preceded by *do* and giving the feature's implementation, states that the actual implementation is postponed (deferred, hence the name) to descendants of class *AIRPLANE*, such as *BOEING_747*.

A feature which is not deferred (that is to say, a fully implemented feature) is said to be **effective**. This terminology carries over to classes: a class is deferred if it has one or more deferred features (even if some of its other features are effective); it is effective if all its features are effective. A deferred class is also called an **abstract class**.

A descendant class that provides an implementation of a feature that it inherits in deferred form is said to **effect** it. For example the class *BOEING_747* effects the feature *lower_landing_gear*; this is graphically represented by the + symbol.

The ++ symbol is reserved for a redefinition: the case in which a class provides a new implementation of a feature that was already effective in the parent; see *lower_landing_gear* for class *BOEING_747_400* on the figure of page 177. These notations come from the BON analysis method (see reference page 38). Effecting and redefinition are the two kinds of redeclaration.

Deferred features and classes have three major applications: providing higher-level abstractions; capturing patterns of behavior; and supporting object-oriented analysis.

The first application is the most common. In applying taxonomical efforts to a certain area, you will usually uncover high-level notions that have no full implementation.

CHUNK in the text-processing system was one such cases; *AIRPLANE* in our latest example is another. But a class that does not have a full implementation can still have many properties worth expressing precisely: features, their preconditions and postconditions, invariants. For example any *CHUNK* will have a command *add_space_after*, although its implementation can only be given in more specific descendants such as *PARAGRAPH* and *FIGURE*; and any *AIRPLANE* will have a *lower_landing_gear* command, characterized by the assertions given above even in the absence of a default implementation.

With polymorphism and dynamic binding, you can declare an entity as being of a deferred type, and rely on dynamic binding to call a feature that is still deferred in the corresponding class:

c: *CHUNK*; *a*: *AIRPLANE*

... Instructions attaching *c to* an effective kind of chunk (a figure or

a paragraph) and *a* to an effective kind of plane (Boeing etc.) ...

c.*add_space_after* (*2.1*);

a.*lower_landing_gear*

The second application is to capture patterns of behavior. This results from the ability of an effective (non-deferred) feature to call deferred ones. The extract introduced earlier under the label "OO-SCHEME" (page 174) could be part of an effective feature:

process is

      -- Solicit the prospect list.

  do

    from

       start

    until

       after

    loop

       item.*marketing_action*

       forth

    end

  end

This feature describes the overall processing quite precisely and hence is effective; but it relies on features such as *marketing_action* that may be deferred. Such a mechanism addresses a major reuse problem: capturing patterns of behavior that are known in their broad outline, but depend on details which may vary. This is again a typical manager's requirement: being able to define an overall strategy and leave details to be filled in later on. One can use the phrase **programs with holes** for such patterns.

The ability to define programs with holes is an essential requirement of ambitious, forward-looking software development: you need to define precisely what you know and want today; but you also need to leave room — the holes — for what will only be known later, and will often have many different variants.

The final application of deferred classes and features is to object-oriented analysis: when studying a system purely for modeling purposes, before any thought about implementation, you may use deferred elements. This will be discussed again in the section on object-oriented analysis (see page 180).

GARBAGE COLLECTION

The execution of an object-oriented system tends to create many objects; some of these objects will eventually become unreachable from the active ones and hence useless.

As noted in chapter 2, advanced implementations of object-oriented languages address this problem by providing an automatic memory management mechanism, or **garbage collector,** that periodically looks for unreachable objects and reclaims their memory.

Although some object-oriented implementations do not offer garbage collection — this is in particular the case with most implementations of hybrid O-O languages such as C++, which make it impossible or very hard to write a safe collector — most experts in the field consider garbage collection to be an essential requirement.

OBJECT-ORIENTED LANGUAGES AND IMPLEMENTATION

The major characteristics of three major object-oriented languages, C++, Eiffel and Smalltalk, were briefly presented in chapter 2; see "OBJECT-ORIENTED LANGUAGES", page 24. The object-oriented examples of this Appendix have used Eiffel syntax.

The earlier discussion also introduced the mechanisms needed to implement O-O languages, and illustrated the notion of object-oriented environment.

OBJECT-ORIENTED ANALYSIS

The object-oriented method is a powerful modeling tool, and in particular can serve right from the beginning of a software effort to perform the requirements analysis of the system under discussion.

Several examples sketched in this chapter have illustrated the idea; text processing classes such are *PARAGRAPH* are typical of the possibilities offered. Here is another (references to which were used in chapter 2).

Assume you are interested in describing certain kinds of chemical plant. Object-oriented modeling means identifying the major object types and organizing the description — the various chapters of the document — around these types, rather than focusing on the functions. The types of interest may include such notions as *PLANT, CONTROL_ROOM, TANK, PIPE, VALVE, VAT* and the like. Each one of them will give a class; since we are at a purely descriptive stage, all these classes will be deferred. But thanks to assertions that does not prevent us from being precise about their properties insofar as we know them. Here for example how class *VAT* might look:

deferred class VAT inherit
    TANK
feature
    fill is
            -- Fill the vat.
      require
        in_valve.open; out_valve.closed
      deferred
      ensure
        in_valve.closed; out_valve.closed; is_full
      end;

    ... [Other features: *is_full, is_empty, empty, in_valve, out_valve,*
      gauge, maximum ...

invariant
    *is_full = (gauge >= .97 * maximum) and (gauge <= 1.03 * maximum)*
end

Inheritance enables us to describe vats as a special case of tanks. Among the features of vats are mechanism to fill a vat (*fill*), find out if it is full (*is_full*) and so on; only *fill* has been detailed. The feature is deferred, of course — this is analysis, not design or implementation — but has precise properties expressed by the assertions: it requires that the input valve be initially open and the output valve closed; it leaves both valves closed and the vat full, in the approximate sense spelled out by the invariant. As in earlier examples, these assertions express a **contract**, a notion that is at least as important at the analysis level as it is for design and implementation:

fill	OBLIGATIONS	BENEFITS
Client	(*Satisfy precondition:*) Input valve must be open, and output valve closed.	(*From postcondition:*) Get the vat in a state in which it is full, with the valves in the proper positions.
Supplier	(*Satisfy postcondition:*) Fill vat and leave the valves in the proper positions.	(*From precondition:*) No need to worry about initial cases in which input valve is closed or output valve open.

Postface

This book benefited from the lessons learned from many people. The books and articles quoted (sometimes critically) in the bibliography sections have set a high standard and provided many ideas. Discussions with countless software project managers have yielded insights and raised tough questions. Many thanks in particular to ISE's customers and to the companies that have relied on our consulting services over the past few years.

Much of the material was taught as part of a seminar series of seminars on Object-Oriented Management, presented in sessions in the US, Canada, Europe, Japan and Australia. The participants' feedback helped refine and extend the presentation.

Talks given at several TOOLS conferences (Technology of Object-Oriented Languages and Systems) by Roger Osmond of Bytex on his experience as O-O project leader have been most enlightening. Other TOOLS invited speakers, in particular Adele Goldberg of ParcPlace, Bob Marcus of Boeing, Meilir Page-Jones of the Wayland Institute, and Donna Veltri of General Electric have been a source of fresh ideas and challenges. A panel at TOOLS USA 94, organized by Eric Aranow on the theme "Reuse: Nature or Nurture?" helped find the proper title for chapter 6.

Jean-Marc Nerson of SOL let me use some of the lessons of his extensive experience of technical and management consulting using object technology, Eiffel and BON. A number of project management insights came from discussions with Philippe Stephan.

The influence of my work at ISE and of the interaction with my colleagues there is visible throughout the book. I should really name all of them, but must at least mention useful comments made by Xavier Le Vourch on the topic of integration and by Eric Bezault on project management.

Kim Waldén, Per Grape, Jean-Marc Éber and Ron House provided criticisms on an earlier draft. James McKim also contributed detailed and useful feedback on both form and content.

I owe to Rock Howard the permission to use ample material from his *Eiffel Outlook* article on the Bytex project (see "A SUCCESS STORY", page 85). I am grateful to Emmanuel Girard for pointing out, many years ago, the relation of Escher's magical waterfall (page 47) to models of the software lifecycle, and to Jacques André of IRISA for providing me with a copy of the non-seamless lifecycle illustration reproduced on page 45.

Index